Nestlé

Nestlé

The Secrets of Food, Trust and Globalization

Friedhelm Schwarz

English translation
by Maya Anyas

KEY PORTER BOOKS

National Library of Canada Cataloguing in Publication Data

Schwarz, Friedhelm
    Nestlé : the secrets of food, trust and globalization

Includes index.
Translation of: Nestlé : Macht Durch Nahrung
ISBN: 1-55263-418-3

1. Nestlé. 2. Food industry and trade. 3. International business enterprises.
I. Title.

HD9015.S94N48 2002   338.7'664   C2002-900752-6

The publisher gratefully acknowledges the support of the Canada Council for the Arts and the Ontario Arts Council for its publishing program.

We acknowledge the financial support of the Government of Canada through the Book Publishing Industry Development Program (BPIDP) for our publishing activities.

Key Porter Books Limited
70 The Esplanade
Toronto, Ontario
Canada M5E 1R2

www.keyporter.com

Electronic formatting: Jean Lightfoot Peters

Printed and bound in Canada

02 03 04 05 06 6 5 4 3 2 1

Contents

Introduction:
More than Coffee and
Chocolate

For five CONSECUTIVE YEARS, Swiss food giant Nestlé SA has been named by *Fortune* magazine as the Most Admired global company in its industry. In the context of the same survey, Nestlé USA has also been cited as the Most Admired American company in the consumer food industry for several years running.

Fortune's annual survey is significant in two ways: First it is a canvass of business insiders who have an intimate knowledge of their industries and who are in a position to provide an informed opinion. Second, the term "most admired" encompasses all aspects of a company's performance, including profitability, long-term value, innovative flair, and managerial proficiency. In addition, a company's commitment to employee development and its sense of responsibility to the larger world must also be factored in.

In all these areas, Nestlé has, by the standards of its peers, excelled. This book takes an in-depth look at Nestlé's activities in all these areas, including marketing to virtually every part of the world and developing appropriate products for dozens of different cultures.

Those products go well beyond the items the company is most noted for, such as Nescafé or KitKat candy bars. Even if you eschew caffeine and chocolate, you probably encounter Nestlé on a daily basis when you drink your Perrier or pop a Stouffer's Lean Cuisine in the microwave. Nestlé's reach also extends into areas such as pet food, eye-care products, and perfume.

But the Nestlé story is also one of people, not products, and one person in particular—its former CEO Helmut Maucher, who in the 1980s and 1990s completed a remarkable turnaround in preserving the fortunes of the world's largest food group.

Maucher's story parallels that of General Electric's legendary CEO Jack Welch in uncanny ways. Both men spent almost their entire working lives in a single corporation and both were handed the leadership of their respective concerns in the year 1980. Both men cleaned up, renovated, and transformed their corporation from top to bottom. Both men hated bureaucracy and both believed that the quality of their staff was the key factor in management. The similarity between the two men extends even to the spectacular success they brought to their corporations, that is, outstanding statistics in steadily increasing profits, sales, and stock values.

Their reputations are not on a par, however. At his recent retirement, Welch was celebrated as the world's best manager. Nothing of the sort took place when Maucher stepped down in the late 1990s. There are several reasons for this difference. The personalities of the two men come to mind first. It is true that while Helmut Maucher was head of Nestlé, he did insist on being Nestlé's sole public representative—he was after all called Mr. Nestlé—however, this policy did not arise from his own nature. He saw public appearances only as part of his duties. He simply did not crave public attention. This was not the case with Jack Welch, whose recent bestseller proves that he is not averse to publicity.

A second reason is the high profile of General Electric in North America. By contrast, the shares of Nestlé are not even traded on any exchanges in the U.S. Finally, while Welch's succession made the front pages of business sections, Maucher's hand-over of the post of Nestlé's CEO to his successor, Peter Brabeck-Letmathe, was managed over a period of years.

In these pages you will meet Maucher and learn the secrets of how he irrevocably altered the course and the culture of Nestlé, and planned for its future. Maucher's approach is still the Nestlé way in its commitment to long-term goals over short-term gains and its reluctance to institute change for change's sake.

No story of Nestlé would be complete without an examination of the controversies the company has faced and still faces. Its marketing of baby formula to the Third World is perhaps the most famous example. But the company also confronts challenges over its decision to use genetically modified ingredients, its production of convenience foods, and its operations in developing countries. I have chronicled all these criticisms as well as Nestlé's response.

Much can be learned from the Nestlé experience, particularly one very timely lesson: Greatness cannot be conjured out of a hat in a few short months. Time still has to be reckoned with, and management and staff need to live both in the future and in the present, if they are to succeed in the long run. If you are looking for achievements that merit recognition and want to learn from the best, Nestlé offers many opportunities for learning.

1

Nestlé,

the Unknown Giant

ALL OVER THE WORLD PEOPLE are buying and consuming Nestlé products without knowing who is behind the brand they have chosen. A full 95 percent of Japanese are under the impression that Nestlé is an indigenous Japanese company. German vacationers are surprised when they encounter Maggi, the quintessentially German condiment, in the most remote corners of the globe. Stouffer's, Lean Cuisine, and Ortega are well-known names in North America; how many consumers are aware that—as Nestlé products—they are closely linked to Toll House, Nesquik, Coffee-mate, and Friskies? Perrier and San Pellegrino, two of the world's best-selling bottled waters, also belong to Nestlé.

It is likely that wherever Nestlé products are sold— and that is all over the world—they are now being consumed by a third generation. This means that most middle-aged people have grown up on Nestlé products. From infant formula and condensed milk to instant coffee, from chocolate and ice cream to yogurt and soup cubes, we regularly meet with Nestlé products in all their variety and diverse labels.

To know Nestlé as it really is, you also have to know something of its history and the mindset of the people who run the corporation. That will be dealt with later in the chapter. First: the products.

Every day, somewhere on the globe, a new Nestlé product or variation is created, or a new name is issued. The six main global brands are Nestlé, Nescafé, Nestea, Maggi, Buitoni, and Purina. In addition there are about 8,500 national and regional brands. Overall, Nestlé realizes 70 percent of its sales from brand name products that stand in either first or second place in their respective market segments.

More than three thousand cups of Nescafé are drunk every second of every day, making it the most popular brand of coffee in the world. Nestlé is also the number-one maker of chocolate drinks and malted drinks, among them Nesquik, Milo, and Nescau. Nestlé owns Taster's Choice instant coffee and the Nestea line of tea products. As well, Nestlé is the world's leading supplier of mineral and spring water. In the United States, for example, Nestlé owns Arrowhead, Poland Spring, Zephyrhills, Deer Park, and Ozarka. Beverages represent, in all, 28.4 percent of Nestlé's sales and—by sales volume—this is the largest section of the corporation's business.

In second position is a category called Milk Products, Nutrition, and Ice Cream, which generates 27 percent of total sales. Here we find the milk formulas for newborns, infants, and children, breakfast cereals, and various pre-pared foods, such as ice cream, yogurt, and nutritional food substitutes. This section also includes supplements that enhance health or boost energy, such as Nestlé's LCI yogurt with acidophilus or Nestlé Omega. Among the well-known brands in this market area are Carnation and PowerBar.

Culinary Products accounts for a further 25.2 percent of total sales. In this category are soups and cooking aids, as well as the Maggi brand of instant noodles. These are sold worldwide, and are adjusted to suit regional tastes in every country. Frozen meals are packaged under brand names such as Stouffer's, Ortega, and Maggi. The Buitoni brand products include not only pasta and sauces but also a wide offering of pizzas and frozen foods. In the European market the corporation offers sausages and other delicatessen items under the Herta name. The company also owns Thomy sauces and salad dressings, as well as Crosse & Blackwell. A subsection known as special activities—think Friskies pet food—rounds out the category.

Chocolate, Sweets, and Biscuits stands in fourth place among product categories, with 13.3 percent of total sales. This includes, along with international brands such as Nestlé, KitKat, Smarties, Lion, Crunch, and After Eight, a multitude of local brands.

But food is not Nestlé's only concern. Pharmaceutical Products constitutes 6.1 percent of total sales, and Nestlé is part owner of L'Oréal, the world leader in cosmetic prod-ucts, a company that owns over five hundred brands and more than two thousand products. Nestlé's subsidiary

Alcon is the world's biggest producer of ophthalmological products, used for eye therapy and eye operations. This company also makes various products for the maintenance of contact lenses.

As this short overview demonstrates, strong brands, a high profile in the markets it enters, and market leadership are the chief attributes of Nestlé's corporate marketing style.

Nestlé is the biggest food producer in the world. At the end of 2001 the corporation employed 236,729 people and managed 479 factories in 84 countries.

This extreme decentralization distinguishes Nestlé from many other global players, which tend to concentrate their production, know-how, and investments in a few strategic locations and to limit their presence on the rest of the globe to marketing and customer service outlets. By contrast, Nestlé expenditures on factories, plants, machinery, and other equipment represent about 4 percent of its sales, a high percentage for the food industry and a sure sign of its involvement abroad.

Worldwide, Nestlé is among the fifty leading corporations, both in terms of its sales and as an employer. Ranked by the value of its stock, at the beginning of January 2000 Nestlé stood in sixty-eighth place among the largest multinationals listed on the stock exchanges of the world. The total stock value of the company was $81.7 billion at year-end 2001. This sum is larger than the gross national product of New Zealand, and indeed of half the countries in which Nestlé maintains production facilities.

Nestlé, the Unknown Giant

Below is a list of the world's largest food producers, as determined by their 2000 food and non-alcoholic beverage sales volume:

- Nestlé (without Ralston Purina), Switzerland, $49.6 billion
- Philip Morris/Kraft (+Nabisco), U.S.A., $35.3 billion
- Unilever (+Bestfoods), Netherlands/Great Britain, $29.2 billion
- Pepsico, U.S.A., $25.5 billion
- Coca-Cola, U.S.A., $20.5 billion
- ConAgra, U.S.A., $20.2 billion
- Mars, U.S.A., $15.0 billion
- Danone, France, $13.2 billion
- General Mills (+Pillsbury), U.S.A., $12.5 billion
- Snow Brand, Japan, $11.2 billion
- Kellogg's (+Keebler), U.S.A., $9.6 billion
- Heinz, U.S.A., $9.4 billion

One has also to realize that the world food market is a very fragmented one: the 20 largest food companies represent only 8.6 percent of it. Despite heavy pressure from the competition, Nestlé has been able to maintain its leading position. Philip Morris, however, moved much closer to Nestlé because its subsidiary, Kraft Foods, acquired about $8.3 billion in sales with the purchase of Nabisco. Unilever also moved closer to the top through the acquisition of $8.6 billion worth of sales from Bestfoods, while General Mills improved its standing by buying up Pillsbury.

It is worth noting that Nestlé stands in second position on the TNI, or Transnationality Index, maintained by the United Nations Conference for World Trade and Development (UNCTAD). This index ranks all transnational corporations and provides a good measure of the degree of globalization of multinationals. Other food producers are far down the list: Unilever in eighth position, the Danone Group SA in twenty-third. Ranked only in terms of its foreign assets, Nestlé is in eleventh position among all multinationals, while its nearest competitors rank twenty-fourth (Unilever) and seventy-eighth (the Danone Group).

Nestlé is the most global concern in its own field, the food industry, with 28 percent of its food product sales generated in emerging markets in Latin America and Asia (14 percent and 15 percent respectively), with 40 percent in Europe and 26 percent in North America. Only Unilever among its main competitors acts in a similarly international manner, with 42 percent of its sales in Europe, 24 percent in North America, 12 percent in Latin America, and 17 percent in the Asia-Pacific region. By contrast, Danone still relies for 62 percent of its sales volume on the European market. Philip Morris, like Nestlé's other U.S. competitors, is still concentrating on its home markets, where 55 percent of its sales are generated. Kellogg's, which includes Keebler, relies for 70 percent of its sales on the North American market, General Mills for 95 percent, and ConAgra for 100 percent.

Nestlé's pre-eminence and global reach has not been achieved without growing pains. At the end of the seventies Nestlé was already a relatively large company, but it lacked an individual profile and sharp outlines. Diversification was the economic fashion of that period: steel mills bought bakeries, energy suppliers invested in hotel chains or in luxury restaurants. Under the Nestlé name too there clustered a colorful bunch of companies and conglomerates, which dealt in the widest array of brands and products. Each unit functioned independently. Some did very well; others did not. Each led an almost separate existence, pursuing its own goals. The only thing that seemed to hold them together was their common ownership.

Nestlé was then forced to make a basic choice. It could reduce the Nestlé Corporation itself into a holding company, breaking it up and making its diverse parts completely independent. Alternatively, it could concentrate on its main products and work on growth in the areas of its core competence. Nestlé chose the latter route, and in so doing secured its future success.

That success during the last twenty years is clearly revealed by the numbers: sales grew by 205 percent between 1980 and 1999. During the same period, net profits climbed 588 percent; they represented 2.6 percent of total sales in 1980, 6.3 percent in 1999, and 7.9 percent in 2001.

Former chairman and CEO Helmut Maucher was the man responsible for the phenomenal growth of Nestlé between 1981 and the end of the millennium. His was a strong personality and he understood both Nestlé's history and the economic trends that were shaping his time. Still, in order to appreciate this crucial period in Nestlé's growth and to judge Maucher's achievement, it is necessary to learn something about the roots of the company.

History does not tell us why, in the year 1830, the pharmacist Heinrich Nestlé moved from his birthplace, Frankfurt am Main, to Vevey on Lake Geneva. What is certain is that the effects of his decision are felt to this day. The center of the enterprise he started has remained in Vevey through all the years of its growth and amalgamation. May 2000 saw the celebration of the completed remodeling of this center, the city's most magnificent structure.

Most large corporations choose to install their headquarters in a large cosmopolitan city; Vevey does not even have an airport. To reach one and connect to international air routes, the traveler first has to go to Geneva, at the other end of the lake. Vevey, however, offers its own unique environment. From anywhere in the city you can see high mountains, their summits snow-covered even in summer, and you can look on the wide expanse and misty horizons of Lake Geneva. On the near shore the climate is Mediterranean, supporting an amazing variety of plant life; above the city are the vineyards, and higher still, Alpine pastures grazed by the famous Swiss cows.

The old town, at the center of Vevey, boasts attractive narrow streets and medieval buildings. The villas of the well-to-do line the promenade along the lake, which still evokes of the turn-of-the-century vacation spot it once was.

The town combines a French lifestyle with Swiss orderliness and an international outlook. If there is a rush hour in Vevey, it never lasts longer than fifteen minutes, and you don't have to sit through more than three red lights before it's over.

Heinrich Nestlé settled in a Vevey that was much smaller than today's city, called himself Henri Nestlé and supported himself as a druggist, selling seeds, mustard, and kerosene lamps. In the year 1857, at the age of forty-three, Nestlé joined with several other Vevey businessmen to found a little enterprise that manufactured two products: a liquid fuel, according to Nestlé's own, never-revealed formula, and artificial fertilizer.

As it happens, Nestlé had other interests as well. Not just an entrepreneur, he also undertook research. As early as 1847 he had set up a private laboratory to find a substitute for mother's milk, in an effort to combat the high mortality rate then prevalent among infants and very young children. He began marketing the result of his research in 1866. It was made of milk, ground grains, and sugar, and was produced through a special drying process. What was new was that Nestlé's process managed to retain most of the ingredients' nutritional value.

The official founding date of the Nestlé firm is considered to be 1866, not just because Henri Nestlé laid the foundation with the introduction of his baby food formula that year, but because another company, the Anglo-Swiss Condensed Milk Company, which was later to merge with Nestlé, was born in 1866.

Since he had no heirs, in 1875, at the age of sixty-one, Henri Nestlé sold his—by then flourishing—enterprise, which was incorporated as Farine Lactée Henri Nestlé. The first few years of this new entity were dedicated to internal reorganization, research to improve product quality, and the creation of new product lines.

The first important milestone in the history of what later became Nestlé was the merger with the Anglo-Swiss Condensed Milk Company in 1905. This concern had been founded in Switzerland by two Americans, the brothers Charles and George Page, and from the outset it was a keen competitor of Nestlé. The Swiss and American mentalities made for a difficult merger of the two companies. However, after some initial disagreements, caused by different corporate cultures and ways of thinking, the two staffs learned to work together. In the process Nestlé became a true transnational company.

Although Nestlé is Swiss in terms of its origins and headquarters, its early merger with an American-run company enabled it to continue to maintain a more American, and thereby more international, point of view. As this book will show, Nestlé continued to acquire and integrate into its culture companies with a strong corporate identity and a long history of their own. There is probably no other commercial concern in the world that would have been able or willing to undertake and successfully complete so many difficult corporate mergers.

In 1929 the company entered the chocolate business through its amalgamation with the Swiss firm Peter,

Cailler, Kohler. In the years that followed, the company developed the world's first soluble instant coffee, which it marketed in 1938 under the name Nescafé.

Although the Great Depression and two world wars curtailed the company's international business activities, its inexorable growth was never halted. By 1946 the Nestlé Group was already manufacturing in no fewer than 107 factories on five continents. The four areas of production at that time were milk products (especially sweetened condensed milk), baby foods, chocolate, and instant beverages.

In 1947 Nestlé's merger with the Swiss firm Alimentana allowed it to enter a new sphere of activity: culinary products. Alimentana had been producing and marketing in many countries, under the name Maggi, a line of soups, bouillon cubes, and spices. Although these food items represented a new departure for Nestlé, the technology involved in their production centered on the same drying process that had been in use at Nestlé for a long time.

The 1950s were characterized by fast internal growth, but not a single new acquisition was undertaken. Nonetheless, the company's turnover in Swiss francs doubled in those ten years, even when inflation is taken into account. Nestlé also expanded its enterprises on all continents.

Nestlé's strategy for the 1960s was three-pronged. First, the company wanted to diversify in the culinary area, in order to offer a wider range of products. Second, Nestlé redoubled its efforts to develop technologies beyond those used to dry its instant products. Third, a worldwide search began for new and growing markets.

Between 1960 and 1974, Nestlé acquired full or part ownership of numerous companies, which meant that its activities now extended to seven major new areas: canned goods, ice cream, frozen foods, chilled foods (such as yogurt), mineral water, restaurants, and California wineries. Business volume increased from $2.5 billion in 1960 to $9.9 billion in 1974.

The acquisitions that led to this phenomenal growth began with the British firm Crosse & Blackwell, which specialized in canned soups and beans. In 1963 came an investment in Libby, McNeill & Libby, the American producer of canned fruit, vegetables, and meats. This partial participation became 100 percent ownership in 1976. Nestlé started in the ice cream business by co-founding a joint company with the French firm France Glaces. To enter into the frozen foods sector Nestlé arranged a merger with Findus International, which was active primarily in Scandinavia and Great Britain.

Nestlé also acquired the American firm Stouffer Corporation.

Vernon Stouffer and his father had founded a restaurant in a suburb of Cleveland, Ohio, in 1924. Since their guests kept asking to take home some of the dishes, they began experimenting with freezing certain hors d'oeuvres and entrees. Business boomed, but for decades it remained within the framework of the restaurant. Not until 1954 did sales reach levels so overwhelming that it was decided to buy a factory specifically for the production of frozen foods.

In 1968, Nestlé bought a minor share of Vittel, the

French mineral water supplier; twenty years later it bought Vittel out completely. Meantime, the corporation acquired Deer Park in the United States and Allan Beverages in Canada. The purchase of West Germany's Blaue Quellen followed in 1974. And in 1992 Nestlé achieved ownership of the glamorous brand Perrier.

The corporation's efforts to diversify led it into the restaurant business in 1970, when it founded Eurest, a joint venture with the Compagnie Internationale des Wagons Lits et du Tourisme. Nestlé also acquired a majority interest in the Australian restaurant chain Cahills. The final move in this diversification process was the purchase of various vineyards and of Beringer Wines, in California. In 1974, still looking to diversify beyond the food sector, Nestlé became part owner of L'Oréal in France. This step seemed to be motivated by the excellent growth potential of the hair care and beauty industry.

The years between 1975 and 1980 saw a contraction of the general economic scene. While the industrialized countries struggled with double-digit inflation, in the developing countries the devaluation of currencies took on downright insane proportions. After the U.S. dollar was taken off the gold standard, all currency exchanges were destabilized and all currencies fell against the Swiss franc.

Over and above all this, the price of the two major raw materials used by Nestlé shot up: the price of coffee increased fourfold, that of cocoa, threefold. Nestlé's sales declined. In 1975 total sales were down to $11.2 billion; in 1979 they recovered somewhat to $13.2 billion.

In 1977, Nestlé bought out Alcon Laboratories, an American company specializing in ophthalmological medications and instruments. What prompted this move was a change in the geographical equilibrium of Nestlé's business activities: sales were growing faster in the developing countries than in the industrialized ones. The corporation sought to redress this imbalance by acquiring a business in a fast-growing sector of the industrialized world. At that time, though Nestlé acted globally, it had not yet begun to *think* in global terms, that is to say in terms of global interrelationships.

There were other problems that confronted Nestlé in the second half of the seventies. In the industrialized countries the earlier brisk growth in consumption slowed down, the economic situation worsened, and competition became tougher. These factors had a negative effect on Nestlé's earnings. In the developing countries growth was rapid, but the economic climate was unstable and risky. Thus the sudden losses suffered in that period by the Argentinian branch of the corporation led to a drop in net earnings, previously at an average of 3.7 percent of sales, to a low of 2.8 percent.

This was the situation when Helmut Maucher took over the leadership of the corporation in 1981.

Helmut Oswald Maucher was born in 1927, in Eisenharz, in the Algäu region of Germany. He completed his schooling in Wangen, graduating as one of the top students in his class. He then entered upon a two-year business apprenticeship in the local dairy, which at that time was already a part of Nestlé. He likes to recall that the contract he signed for this apprenticeship was the only written agreement ever made between him and Nestlé during his long career with the company. (It is indeed not customary for Swiss firms to issue written contracts to their employees. None of the current executives of Nestlé has a written contract that stipulates their salary, vacation, pension, or other benefits.)

In 1951 Maucher went to work for Nestlé in Frankfurt as a commercial clerk. In Frankfurt he also pursued further education, studying business, economics, and law. By the time he obtained his MBA, he was working in Purchasing for Nestlé Germany. His career at Nestlé continued to flourish during the next two decades. He became head of marketing for Nestlé Germany and manager of Findus-Jopa before leaving Nestlé because of internal disagreements in 1970. He joined the Hamburg Co-op, a large organization, but was invited to rejoin Nestlé in 1972.

In October 1980, Helmut Maucher, who was then head of Nestlé Germany, became a member of the executive committee, a triumvirate that essentially ran the corporation together with the CEO. In November 1981, Maucher was elected to the board of directors of Nestlé SA. He managed Nestlé in tandem with the other two members of the executive committee until it was disbanded in 1986. From then on Helmut Maucher was in sole control of Nestlé as its chief executive officer. In 1990 Maucher also became chairman of the board.

Within three or four years Maucher was able to increase

the liquidity of the corporation to the point where further acquisitions and growth became possible. Already he recognized the significance of scale. "In many sectors you simply have to be large and global to ensure your survival," he has remarked. With this understanding Maucher concentrated on making Nestlé the largest food supplier in the world. By 1996 he had achieved his aim.

He began to carry out his plan in 1983, when Nestlé bought out several smaller concerns in the areas of food, chocolate, and cosmetics. At about the same time Maucher decided to enter the roasted coffee business, and to this end he acquired some small companies in Canada, Sweden, and Spain. Among Maucher's biggest coups was the 1985 takeover of the Carnation Company, the giant U.S. maker of milk products, pet food, and culinary products. He paid what was at that time the monumental sum of $3.5 billion. In 1988, Nestlé made two other big acquisitions, buying Rowntree-Mackintosh, the fourth-largest chocolate and confectionery producer in the world, and Buitoni-Perugina, Italy's third-largest food corporation.

Another important step taken in 1988 was a change in the bylaws of the corporation to allow foreigners to buy Nestlé's registered shares. These registered shares accounted for two-thirds of Nestlé's entire capital in stocks (now 100 percent), and until then only Swiss citizens were allowed to own them.

In 1990, Nestlé linked up with General Mills to form a joint subsidiary to handle their breakfast cereals business, Cereal Partners Worldwide SA, headquartered in Morges,

Switzerland. In the same year the corporation signed a long-term contract for a partnership with the Walt Disney Corporation. With this agreement Nestlé became the exclusive purveyor of food and drinks in all Disney restaurants and amusement parks. Nestlé also obtained the exclusive right to use Walt Disney figures on its packaging and in its advertising in Europe and in the Near and Far East. Other acquisitions by Maucher included the mineral water producing group Perrier in 1992 and Alpo pet food in 1994.

Looking back, Maucher remarks: "I had the courage or the single-mindedness to change things, when most of those around me had not yet understood the lay of the land. Of course, sometimes it helps to have the sheer power to be able to say: now, we are going ahead with this."

Maucher also had the experience of what happens when one does *not* have power. There are examples of this during his first years at Nestlé, when he was an assistant manager; his suggestions were rejected because he was too young and lacked an influential position. "When I was a very young employee, back in Germany, I had suggested that Nestlé should enter the cereal business. Kellogg had sales of 13 million German marks, as long as forty-five years ago. At that time I told Nestlé, 'Go into the cereal business, it has a great future.' My main argument was that for the raw materials of this business, you do not need to make the detour through the animal ... Nestlé would not enter into cereals at that time, because all they had in their heads was milk, chocolate, and coffee.

27

"Once I was in Vevey, I did what I could to rectify this error. Since we were twenty years behind, I entered into a joint venture with General Mills, and managed to get the Nestlé logo onto the packages. By now it is common knowledge that breakfast cereals, from muesli to dry cereal, constitute a successful, worldwide business."

The young Maucher also tried unsuccessfully to get Nestlé into the pet food business, something he finally achieved with the 1985 acquisition of Carnation. "At the time I bought Carnation," he notes, "some Swiss people said, 'Our Swiss mountain altitude has gone to the head of that German.' It happened to be the largest takeover ever made by a European company with respect to an American competitor."

By 2001, Nestlé was number one in the realm of pet foods. Peter Brabeck, successor to Helmut Maucher as Nestlé's CEO, acquired Ralston Purina for $10.3 billion and merged it with Nestlé's Friskies branch to form Nestlé Purina Pet Care. This new enterprise has annual sales of $6.3 billion.

Helmut Maucher emphasizes how important it was for him to listen to his hunches. He could see the changes that were coming and knew that it was crucial for Nestlé to achieve completely new dimensions in order to prepare itself: "I completed all the acquisitions for Nestlé before the others even began, before all the papers were full of mergers, before the banks had opened special investment departments. We completed 80 percent of our homework before the competition even got off the ground. The others only got started when everything had already gone up in price, when the competition had become quite insane."

In a world of corporate heavyweights it is essential to get in the first punch. "Whatever *we* have, our competition, say Unilever, has as well," says Maucher. "Their staff is as professional as ours. They know their marketing instruments as well as we do. Their technological experience is solid ... So how are we different? We are better in that we have a few people with better vision, people who can marshal the power, the quality, the commitment, and the motivation to carry through their vision. Only in these two areas can we differentiate ourselves: in vision and the ability to translate it into action. In all other areas the differences are marginal."

2

Nestlé's Tripartite Division of the World

T O MEET THE CHALLENGES involved in being the world's most successful purveyor of food, Nestlé has developed a unique management structure that maximizes the strengths of both headquarters and its troops on the ground. Call it a matrix of efficiency. It is organized along two axes, which are interpenetrating: the Functional Axis and the Regional Axis.

The Functional Axis includes two major elements: Strategic Business Units (SBUs) and Technology and Production/Research and Development. This axis is responsible for planning all important product-related strategies and for making all major decisions with respect to products. It also provides effective support to the national branches in all the regional zones concerning products— their manufacture, packaging, or marketing. Thus Nestlé effectively promotes the exchange of information across national boundaries. The Functional Axis also includes core activities like finance and the comptroller, marketing, human resources, and corporate affairs.

The Strategic Business Units deal with major areas of food production: Milk and Milk Products, Coffee/Beverages, Chocolate/Confections/Crackers, Ice Cream, Food, Food Services and Pet Care. Nestlé CEO Peter Brabeck has chosen to retain personal control of the Strategic Business Unit for nutrition, and he also directs the water business, which is being run independently of the other Nestlé units out of Paris, such as Nestlé Waters. The whole area of pharmaceuticals and cosmetics also lies outside this corporate model.

Research and Development are centrally managed, and are assigned to the sphere of Technology and Production. This area also covers Quality Management; Engineering/Packaging; Industrial Performance/Factory Systems; Environment/Regulatory Affairs; Agriculture; Intellectual Asset Management; and Technical Personnel Co-ordination. R & D is carried out in the Nestlé Research Centre, the Product Technology Centers, and the Research and Development Centers. Included here, but in a special position, is Nestlé Nepresso SA, which prepares, packages, and sells coffee exclusively to produce espresso coffee.

For years Nestlé managers everywhere were mainly generalists, which proved a disadvantage when the competition used regional expertise. To correct this condition the Nestlé Group decided to provide centralized specialists to aid the managers in the regions; the establishment of the strategic units was the result.

The strategic units form a link with the operational units in the various markets. Whereas the heads of the geographical zones manage a staff of experts on national and regional markets, the SBUs provide specialists in certain products as well as marketing and technological experts. The interplay of these different dimensions makes for synergies that can far outperform any purely geographical planning.

Fritz Wieshofer was one of these SBU specialists until 2001. His current duties include identifying general consumer trends and translating them into suggested strategies for management. He explains this challenge not only in terms of what should be done but, even more important, what should be avoided. The idea is to learn from mistakes and misjudgments in other areas, and to not repeat them.

One of the things the leader of an SBU has to do is work closely with the markets, making sure that the measures that have been decided on are in fact implemented. Wieshofer's motto is "Make it happen." He knows that for ideas to be realized, constant guidance and support are needed. The one thing to keep in mind at Nestlé, as one is making adjustments to products, is that the core concept of a brand should never be diluted.

Along the Regional Axis there are three geographic zones. These are the areas into which Nestlé has divided the map of the world. Nestlé's partition of its global business into zones applies only to foods and beverages, excluding bottled water, which constitute 81 percent of the Nestlé Group's sales. The three zones are Europe (total sales 31.6 percent), the whole of North and South America (total sales 31.4 percent), and Asia, Oceania, and Africa (total sales 18.3 percent). (The remaining 18.7 percent, "Other Activities," comprises the water business, pharmaceutical products, and CPW, the joint venture with General Mills in breakfast cereals.)

The picture changes when we look at profits. The European food business, accounting for 25.2 percent of profits, brings in less than the Americas, which account for 31.9 percent. Asia, Oceania, and Africa contribute 23.5 percent of the corporation's total profits. The zones differ not only in respect to net profits but also in profitability, that is, the ratio of sales to profits. This is lowest in Europe and highest in Asia, Oceania, and Africa.

Nestlé's thirteen most important individual markets line up as follows, expressed in billions of U.S. dollars:

United States	12.4	Brazil	2.1
France	4.7	Spain	1.5
Germany	4.0	Canada	1.0
Great Britain	2.8	Philippines	.9
Italy	2.4	Switzerland	.8
Japan	2.3	Australia	-0.9
Mexico	2.2		

Growth rates in these countries vary tremendously, of course, and depend also on what happens to the local currency. Expressed in Swiss francs, in the year 2001 they ranged from +10.3 percent for Switzerland to –11.1 percent for Japan. However, in local currency the setback in Japan was transformed into +0.8 percent. In the United States sales increased in terms of Swiss francs by 7.5 percent, but in terms of dollars by 7.9 percent. In Canada a growth rate of +5.0 percent was registered, but in Canadian dollars the change was +9.8 percent.

Before looking at markets in detail, it is important to note the significance of Nestlé as a Swiss company. Switzerland is very small, and today its home market contributes only marginally to Nestlé's overall sales, with 1.5 percent taking place there. Since the Swiss market is so tiny, any Swiss company that plans to grow has to cross the national border right from the start.

This simple fact has had a lot to do with Nestlé's becoming a global corporation with multinational management. How well a company has adjusted to global needs is best judged by looking at how many different nationalities are represented on its top management team. As of April 1, 2000, all the top positions at Nestlé USA were held by so-called expatriates, employees who have worked in other parts of the world. No other corporation has a leadership team with such wide horizons.

Europe, small though it is, still plays an important role in the Nestlé Group. It contributed $15.9 billion to food and beverage turnover and $1.7 billion in trading profits in 2001. Of course, Nestlé has been making and selling food in Europe since the founding of the company. The European zone today supports 194 factories.

European growth rates are lower than those in other areas. Robert Raeber, who was head of the European zone until his retirement in 2001, points out that the very fact that Nestlé products are so well established there makes them less interesting: they lack novelty value. Europeans do not buy Nestlé to find out about the products.

For any one of the large European countries, Nestlé's product line will encompass about four thousand products, but only forty or fifty of these are for sale in *all* of Europe. This small, select group of products is also available worldwide. It includes KitKat, the chocolate bar, Lion, Perrier, and S. Pellegrino.

Most food items vary from country to country, as does coffee. Consumer preferences for the latter product diverge most markedly among Europeans. They all seem to disagree on blend, roast, and other aspects of what constitutes a good cup of coffee. Thus Nescafé has adjusted to local tastes, while the same brand name is retained everywhere.

Nestlé's CEO, Peter Brabeck, does not expect this arrangement to change, even since the European market is strengthened by a common currency. "You cannot regionalize or globalize food products and consumer preferences. These things cannot be standardized by artificial means. On the contrary, we find a much more intricate segmentation of markets now than there was twenty years ago."

Raeber says: "When it comes to food and drink, Old Europe has become a bit tired; consumers there do not consider food to be a central issue any more. Most Europeans are now overfed. Quantity has ceased to matter; growth can be achieved only through quality, and through quick adjustments to the constantly changing habits of consumers."

What the European consumer wants is supplementary benefits from food, such as food items that promote good health or provide more convenience. Then there is the trend towards ever smaller families. Today, over half of all European households consist of only one person. Naturally, consumer habits have changed dramatically as a result. Food eaten outside the home now accounts for 30 percent of food consumption, and the trend is growing. This also means that the role of grocery stores in food sales is contracting, while restaurants and places that sell snacks are taking over more and more of the food business. One result of shrinking household size is that the size of packages tends to diminish, from, say, four servings per package to one or two.

"For concerns like Nestlé, the European Union, with its common market, offers great advantages," Raeber comments. "The flow of goods is guaranteed, so it is really possible to manufacture without regard to location." The introduction of the euro is a great help, says Raeber, because it removes all considerations of currency from the choice of manufacturing sites. The only currency that has to be calculated in relation to the euro is the British pound.

Nestlé is also looking to expand into eastern Europe. The company took immediate advantage of the end of the Cold War, entering the new markets of Russia, the Ukraine, and Belarus in the early 1990s. The first steps were taken through agencies, but Nestlé now owns twenty-four factories in eastern Europe and perceives great growth potential there. At the moment, however, this is limited by the populations' reduced buying power. In this respect there are considerable differences within eastern Europe. Whereas buying power in Russia is still very restricted, in Poland, Hungary, Slovakia, Romania, and the former Yugoslavia, consumer spending is approaching the pattern of the rest of Europe. One great advantage for Nestlé as a producer is that in the eastern European markets the corporation can use the same outlets it has been partnering with in the West.

In the Asia, Oceania, and Africa zone, Nestlé had sales of $9.2 billion in 2001, and made $1.5 billion in trading profit. Economically speaking, Japan is as large as a whole continent, and its market is therefore extremely important. Nestlé enjoys a very special position there. It built its first Japanese factory in 1936. Brabeck says that the business Nestlé built in Japan has been very successful and that it is now able to enter a diversification phase. This means there will be more emphasis on pet foods, the water business, and chocolates and sweets.

In the next few years sales in the countries of Southeast Asia will grow in sheer volume. On average Brabeck expects an 8 to 10 percent increase in sales volume. To ensure efficient delivery of products to the markets in this region, manufacturing is being carried out on a narrow, regional basis.

Nestlé has been active in China for a long time, and now owns eighteen factories there. The Chinese market has begun to show profits, but the first few years were very difficult in terms of investment. Growth is now measured in double figures.

Brabeck still counts India, including the whole subcontinent, among the difficult markets, though Nestlé is gaining some growth there as well. It is likely that India's full growth potential has not yet been reached. Brabeck sees the problem in India as essentially political. Indians have an ambivalent attitude towards foreign investors. Somewhere deep in the nation's subconscious there still linger strong reservations, which do not permit India to stand wholeheartedly behind companies like Nestlé. In this, India is very different from, say, China, where the government endorsed Nestlé's investments from the beginning, repeatedly removing serious obstacles in Nestlé's path.

In the Americas, Nestlé grossed $3.2 billion in 2001; trading profit amounted to $2.1 billion. Nestlé was exporting food products to both North and South America as early as 1880. In 1920 it built a factory in Brazil. Others followed in Argentina, Mexico, and Chile. By the beginning of the 1950s, Nestlé had a manufacturing presence in all South American countries. Today, Nestlé is the leading food producer in South America.

When Nestlé started making condensed milk in South America in the 1920s, it worked with many small suppliers. Nestlé provided technical support to these farmers, to increase milk production. Today, many of these same suppliers are in their third generation of working with Nestlé. Nestlé always proceeded in the same way: common interests bound the company to local suppliers, and often to whole communities, cities, or even countries. In Argentina, for example, people consider Nestlé to be a member of the family, and this is important in an area where great significance is attached to good relations with all social circles.

The current overseer of the Americas zone is one of Nestlé's executive vice-presidents, Carlos E. Represas. He began as a marketing trainee at the Nestlé Company in White Plains, New York, in 1968, and his subsequent career ultimately led him, through various positions in Brazil, Spain, Ecuador, Venezuela, and Mexico, to the top of the corporation. What seems especially pleasing to Represas is that he, a Mexican, is in charge of the American market, which from the point of view of Mexico always seems vastly superior. He feels that his example will encourage Mexicans to look north, not just with awe or envy, but also with the intention of using their qualifications to build careers for themselves.

Represas is adamant that if you want to be the leading food producer in the world, you have to be the leader in the United States. "For three years in a row the real internal growth of Nestlé in the U.S. has been above the Group average, and that is the most competitive market in the world. Today we are the number two food manufacturer in the U.S. [after Philip Morris]." As he talked about Nestlé's expansion within this important area, Represas repeated the words of Nestlé managers in many different positions and places: "It is people who make the difference. And people have to adjust their actions to worldwide trends."

Many new products originate in the American market, enter the world market from there, and go on to register great success. Of course, products from elsewhere can conquer the United States market as well. The coffee whitener Coffee-mate started as an American product but is now popular around the world. Another typical American product is the chocolate bar Nestlé Crunch. By contrast, Stouffer, the country's largest frozen-food producer, with sales of $1.7 billion, achieved its greatest American success with Skillet Sensations, a line of ready-to-eat foods that are made with technology developed in Europe.

According to Represas, the United States is also the most innovative market in the world. "I have not seen any society in my life," he says, "that has [as much] capacity to change as American society." In Represas' view, you have to take into account all the directions and opportunities available in the U.S. before you can study the rest of the globe.

In this regard the United States' northern neighbor, Canada, is also important. The sheer size of the U.S. precludes much detailed testing. But, according to Represas, with one-tenth the population, Canada represents "a laboratory for Nestlé. We have tried and tested a lot of things in Canada."

Through its research Nestlé has identified three distinct North American food trends. First, convenience products are gaining in importance. Second, young consumers especially are more and more interested in nutritional food products—what Nestlé calls the "good for you" dimension—and they also drink a lot more water. The third trend is that people are moving away from dieting and are looking at ordinary foods to give them a balanced diet.

No one doubts the prime importance of the North

American market in terms of the world economy. The 270 million inhabitants of the United States and the 30 million in Canada are extraordinarily enthusiastic consumers, and they are among the best-paid ones on the globe. North America contains a multiplicity of cultures and lifestyles; and it is interesting to meet the challenges offered by North Americans as a group, who are more willing to embrace change, and more rapid in their adoption of new products, than any other consumers. This exuberance, once the hallmark of the culturally diverse urban, coastal regions of the continent, long ago came to characterize the populations of the cities in the heartland as well.

If there is any truth to the idea that cultural identity is most obviously manifested in cuisine, then so-called "crossover cuisine" is surely one of the best proofs of the proverbial American spirit of progress. In the United States it is not unusual to find, for example, elements of French cuisine combined in imaginative ways with ideas from North African, Mediterranean, and oriental cooking. In Europe, where cross-over cuisine is still in the experimental stages, such exotic accents added to traditional local cuisine would be looked on with suspicion. Yet in the United States and Canada this variety of tastes is offered not only in exclusive eating places but quite routinely on the food pages of the daily newspaper and in the frozen-food section of the supermarket.

It is impossible to understand the Nestlé Corporation without knowing how it functions in North America, the largest contiguous market in the world. Nestlé differs tremendously from other European companies in terms of the corporation's attitude to doing business in North America. Very few European companies take advantage of the opportunities offered by this market. For example Droege & Comp., a management consulting firm, determined that only 40 percent of German businesses make any effort to increase their turnover by venturing into the United States. The same applies to businesses in other European countries.

Certainly, Nestlé has a long history in North America. The first factory Nestlé built on this continent was in Fulton, New York, in 1907. At first, only milk products and cheese were manufactured there, but in 1939 Nestlé made its first move in its love affair with the American public, when it introduced Toll House Morsels to the market. With the introduction of these popular chocolate chip cookies, Nestlé became a part of the baking tradition of North America.

The next big step came in 1948 with the marketing of Nestlé's "Quik" chocolate powder. A third generation of Americans is now growing up with this instant drink, which in 1999 was renamed Nesquik, a name it now bears around the world.

The Nestlé Corporation's tradition of American success is only in part the result of the chocolate side of the business. Undoubtedly more important has been Nestlé's carefully planned acquisition policy, which extends beyond North America and might be called its policy of "buying tradition." The takeover of Stouffer's has already been noted. In 1985, Nestlé acquired Carnation, a concern with roots that reach back to the year 1899. Nestlé's acquisitions in other countries were also aimed at buying tradition: in 1988 the corporation bought out Buitoni in Italy, a company that was founded in 1827, and in 1995 it acquired Ortega Mexican Foods, a company that started doing business in 1897 under its founder, Emilio Ortega.

In each case Nestlé's management chose a firm with a mentality that resembled its own, with the intention of facilitating the mergers and maintaining the Nestlé culture. Of course there were other acquisitions as well, but in the majority of cases Nestlé chose to ally itself with cultures and traditions as close to its own as possible.

Traditional feelings are particularly significant when we consider Nestlé's achievement in making its brands a component of North American heritage. Every new product under the umbrella of Nestlé chocolates, of Carnation milk products, or of Stouffer's frozen foods can lay claim to the tradition of these corporations for good quality and reliability. This is important, for no matter how open-minded North American consumers are, they respect history and appreciate the roots and background of the products they buy as a part of their overall quality.

It would be a serious mistake to conclude from all this that Nestlé's success is based solely on tradition. It is also of tremendous significance that the management techniques at Nestlé USA have been very unusual and innovative.

Joe Weller, chairman and chief executive officer of Nestlé USA, began his career in 1968, the same year as

Carlos Represas. It is true that he did not start at Nestlé but at the corporation's then competitor, the Carnation Company. In 1985, the year of the merger, Joe Weller was executive vice president at Carnation World Headquarters, responsible for pet foods, dairy products, and food services. After moving to Nestlé, Weller gained international experience as head of its Australia operation. He stepped into his present position in 1995.

Weller's innovations at Nestlé USA have been most marked in the area of teamwork. The clearest indication of the importance he attaches to the team is a move he initiated at the beginning of 2001: the executive offices on the twenty-first floor of the Nestlé headquarters in Glendale, California, were all turned into meeting rooms. All the managers moved to other floors, to be with their teams. This was no symbolic change; it was a move to lend practical support to the various teams by putting their leaders right in their midst. You cannot be a part of a team if you are not present. Today, on the twenty-first floor, all are free to visit a recently installed art show.

Joe Weller also uses a "Blueprint for Success," which he created to serve as the basis for change. Much more than a mission statement, the blueprint addresses in detail the issues involved in change, listing what's in and what's out. Typical contrasts include: "balance" (in) vs. "all work and no play" (out); "personal accountability" (in) vs. "it's not my job" (out); "leveraging the global knowledge of Nestlé" (in) vs. "thinking we have all the answers" (out); and "time to think creative" (in) vs. Friday meetings after 10 a.m. (out).

Each of these points is practiced by Weller personally. For example, he enjoys breaking into meetings after 10 a.m. on Fridays in order to remind the staff that it is time to end it. Another change he has instituted is Nestlé's "always casual" clothing policy. This was one rule that the majority of his co-workers greeted with a sigh of relief. Weller argues that motivation and creativity do not arise from ties or dark suits, so there is no point in maintaining this attire.

The most successful component of Nestlé USA is the Prepared Foods Division, 90 percent of whose production consists of frozen foods. The spectacular success of frozen foods is not solely the result of the corporation's marketing techniques; it is also due to changes in consumers' eating habits and lifestyles.

Some of these important changes are not recent. The time-saving weekly mega-shopping trip has been used by American families for many years. Better refrigeration allows consumers to take advantage of the fact that food is most conveniently and compactly stored in frozen form. An even more fundamental change is that the majority of Americans now have very little time for cooking. Frozen, ready-to-eat foods offer an acceptable alternative to fast-food restaurants. Cooking in the U.S. has become a luxury, a hobby that can be pursued only on weekends.

One reason for this is that the structure of the North American family has changed. Only 6 percent of families now conform to the classic ideal, with a male breadwinner and a stay-at-home mother. Women in general tend to be caught between career and home. As a result, "cooking" is now defined as maintaining a balanced diet by reheating various commercially prepared foods. No wonder, then, that products like Stouffer's Skillet Sensations have been such runaway successes. Quality is a key factor: food writers in American gourmet magazines routinely give Nestlé good marks, especially for the high quality of its products.

Although much has changed, tastes have remained largely the same. The old best-seller among frozen dishes was macaroni and cheese, and this continues to be the case. If in the past single portions were what was most often demanded, today there is an ever-growing need for large packages that furnish a meal for four to six people.

Fortunately for the consumer, cooking in the Nestlé factories is still done in the traditional way, though in much larger quantities than in the past. Mashed potatoes are cooked in the classic manner: potatoes are peeled, chopped, and boiled; then they are puréed with huge beaters. The dishes are still hot when they are moved into the automatic freezing installations.

BURLINGTON, WI: CHOCOLATE CITY USA

Burlington, Wisconsin, is a lovely place to live and work. Until 1985, however, this fact was not generally appreciated. That year the citizens decided that a large annual event would be a good way to capture the attention of people in the surrounding areas. The idea of the Chocolate

Festival arose naturally from the fact that Nestlé USA's Chocolate & Confections Division happened to be the town's largest employer.

The first such festival took place in March 1986, and attracted a respectable crowd of 20,000 visitors to the town of barely 9,000 inhabitants. Today, over 100,000 people come to "Chocolate City USA" in order to participate in the annual Chocolate Fest. Nestlé is one of the main sponsors of the event. A huge chocolate sculpture forms the main attraction and symbolizes the theme of each year's festival.

What matters for Nestlé, however, is to show how deeply and securely the corporation is rooted in local society and its traditions. This has not changed since 1965, when the chocolate factory first opened. At that time Nestlé was already familiar with regional conditions through the activities connected with its milk business, while local dairy farmers and other suppliers were acquainted with Nestlé's business principles through the same connections. Within the region, Burlington was chosen for its rail connection and proximity to interstate highways.

The success of the Chocolate Festival provoked the usual attacks from envious competitors. For example, Hershey's Chocolates tried very hard, though unsuccessfully, to block the town's official designation as Chocolate City USA. The city finally proved that it was not trying to promote Nestlé products, but only to bring Burlington itself some much-needed publicity.

Anyone who wishes to understand the business philosophy of Nestlé should begin with a visit to the Burlington chocolate factory. This can be very enlightening, since this site embodies the basic manufacturing operation, far removed from the international business, untouched by marketing, and nowhere near any customers. The emphasis here is primarily on product quality, efficiency, and reduced costs. According to plant manager Peter K. Ferris, the key to these three areas of success is held by the workers at the plant.

Ferris has been making chocolate in every conceivable shape and flavor for thirty-four years. A tall man with close-cropped hair, he is a hands-on manager who knows every detail of his plant. He has always used the same traditional ingredients: cocoa beans, milk, and sugar. Based on his years of experience Ferris is convinced that the process of improvement is a continuous one.

"A chocolate factory is nothing but a huge kitchen," says Ferris. This means first of all cleanliness and hygiene. These twin concerns are applied throughout the plant, starting at the entrance to the factory's warehousing units. In the past, raw materials, which are delivered in containers, were moved on wooden skids. This traditional warehouse storage system allows forklifts to move and lift heavy boxes easily. One day, however, tiny wood particles were detected in some finished products and traced to these wooden skids. How the slivers got into the packages is not known, but the result was that wooden skids were banned from the warehouse, new ways were developed to stack cartons, and the forklifts were adjusted to fit these new systems. A huge investment to remove a small problem? Certainly it might look like that to an outsider. However, according to Ferris, you can only maintain perfect quality if you act promptly to protect it.

There are two ways in which a chocolate factory differs markedly from a kitchen in a home, restaurant, or bakery. One of these is that chocolate is made here. Since standards are very high nowadays, it has become impossible to produce chocolate of completely consistent quality in any but a large industrial context. For this reason even the finest bakeries and the makers of the most exquisite truffles must fall back on industrially prepared chocolate. The consistent quality of bulk chocolate does not depend only on the raw materials used, but on control of the processes of production as well.

The criteria here are consistency and safety. Although it may still be possible to mill your own flour or roast coffee beans in small machines at home, cocoa beans cannot be processed in small, non-industrial settings, just as fresh milk has to be prepared and treated with concern for the safety of those who will partake of it. These processes require expensive equipment and a lot of technical knowledge.

The other difference between a chocolate factory and any other kitchen is that in the factory nothing is thrown away; there is no waste. What cannot be used is sold to another business.

Here is an interesting point to ponder: at the present time, the rage in global quality control is Six Sigma, the method introduced by Jack Welch at General Electric. This is a method for improving productivity by radically reducing the error rate in products, services, and processes. "Six Sigma" means a rate of error of 3.4 per million. This can be expressed in terms of a degree of perfection equivalent to 99.9996 percent. Using this matrix, in May 2001 Ferris's factory showed a standard of quality of 99.9980 percent.

While some corporations may regard Six Sigma as representing a vision of a whole new world of quality, at Nestlé this level of quality control has been practiced for years. Each worker has known for a long, long time exactly what factors have an impact on the quality of the products he deals with. Each worker also knows that it is his/her duty to keep an eye on these factors and find and suggest ways for further improvements. No compromise is ever allowed in an effort to achieve short-term gains. Details are always in the foreground of everyone's attention, and each worker knows that quality is the foundation on which the company must base all decisions to increase efficiency or reduce costs.

Safety in the workplace is an integral aspect of a high-quality production as far as Ferris is concerned. Even a small accident, such as a sprained ankle because someone stumbled over a step, is regarded by Ferris as an avoidable expense and an unnecessary delay. The accident rate at the chocolate factory fell from 65 in 1999 to 41 in 2000.

Another aspect of the Burlington chocolate factory is typical of Nestlé operations worldwide: of the 528 workers, 35 percent have been with the company for over twenty years, and another 32 percent for over fifteen years. Continuity and long-range planning are a basic necessity if a company is going to learn from its experience and from that of its staff, and thereby achieve continuous change and constant improvement. These are the strengths of the Old Economy as against the New Economy.

3

Nestlé's Recipe for Success:
The Maucher Legacy

I F YOU LOOK AT A CORPORATION that has been out-standingly successful over a period of years or decades, your investigation will invariably lead you to a person. This person will always turn out to have had a crucial impact on the business, contributed new ideas of lasting importance, demonstrated an ability to translate these ideas into action, and inspired his or her fellow workers. Very often it is the gifted founder of the company—an inventor or a brilliant salesperson—who plays this role, but not always.

An outstanding individual at the helm of an enterprise is rare. Such people do not surface frequently, nor do they always appear at the right time. This is proven by the lasting influence of great men in organizations: they can exert power for half a century beyond their time of active participation.

Such personalities need to find themselves in an environment that offers special leadership opportunities. A manager, however talented, rarely has a chance to reveal his abilities in an already flourishing enterprise that is not facing any major internal or external problems of any kind. By the same token, being the immediate successor to a great leader is not the best milieu in which to show one's own superior mettle.

It is not even enough to be the right person in the right place at the right time. A leader also needs sufficient time to plant her ideas in the heads of all her managers and then into those of other co-workers. That sort of thing cannot be done by fiat. It takes conviction and persistent, long-term, daily practice.

For about twenty years Nestlé was managed by a person who, during his tenure, was able to accomplish the following organizational changes:

- initiating a broadly based and continuous process of improvement
- instilling easy-to-understand values in the workforce
- directing the corporation to respect people and their needs
- focusing the enterprise on achieving profits through good management

Chapter One has shown just how successful Helmut Maucher was in fulfilling this mandate. To reiterate: from 1980 to 1999 Nestlé's sales grew by 205 percent and net profits more than doubled. Moreover, Maucher redirected Nestlé back to its core competencies and created a new and enduring management structure. These are the achievements of an exceptional manager and an exceptional leader.

The road to such success was sometimes bumpy. Reviewing the activities of Maucher's tenure, one can find some decisions he made that did not bring about the desired results, or did not bring them within the time frame he predicted. For example, in acquiring Perrier, Maucher underestimated the strength of the CGT, its communist-run union, and misjudged the sympathies of the French Ministry of Labor. In the meantime, the labor disputes have been settled and, as of 2001 Perrier was again profitable.

In another case, at the German firm Herta Fleisch und Wurstwaren, Maucher's original strategy to absorb the meat giant had to be changed. Instead, he was obliged to sell certain parts of this large enterprise, including all slaughtering and meat processing operations. To make the acquisition profitable, Nestlé had to concentrate solely on the production of Herta convenience foods.

In a similar vein, a 1990 joint venture with Coca Cola came a cropper. Maucher admits that he failed to appreciate the extent of the bottling company's conservatism. He was taken aback at their refusal to extend the range of their products, as they finally insisted that they had sufficient sales with their core product, Coke. Eventually, the deal was revived in a more modest form, which confines co-operation to ready-to-drink tea and coffee products to be marketed in twenty-four countries, as well as an agreement on a future line extension into drinks based on herbal formulas. The new corporation, Beverage Partners Worldwide, has set up its headquarters in Zurich, Switzerland. With their expanded offerings the partners are looking to achieve an annual business volume of 250 million cases of drinks. Thus it seems that the pioneering efforts of Helmut Maucher will bear fruit after all, even if it is ten years after he had to give up on this scheme.

These setbacks did not affect the general course of Maucher's leadership at Nestlé. For over two decades Helmut Maucher personified the company; he was known the world over as "Mr. Nestlé." In the words of current CEO Peter Brabeck: "Helmut Maucher made a decision to make Nestlé into the world's leading food producer and to differentiate it from its competitors. We had two choices at that point. We could remain a conglomerate, which had been the management goal of the preceding administration. They had diversified into hotels, restaurants, wineries, the pharmaceutical business, and also bought into L'Oréal. This had been a very expensive plan. And then Maucher came along and said: forget the whole thing, I am convinced that Nestlé can be great if the corporation concentrates on food production. That, in my opinion, was Maucher's most important and most risky decision."

Maucher recalls the gist of what he told his staff: "We want to serve the whole world, but we do not want to be the same as all the rest of the world. We want to be in a business that we actually know something about." So Nestlé began concentrating on food production. Certain profitable capital investments in the areas of dietary, ophthalmological, and cosmetic products were retained, however. As it later turned out, these investments paid off through synergies in the realm of research.

While cutting back in extraneous areas, Maucher also began introducing measures to rationalize the firm's operations. So, at the same time as costs were cut, Maucher began investing in research, marketing, and management training. He improved the flow of information from the company's many markets while simplifying the bureaucratic process at central headquarters, especially in the area of human resources.

Maucher himself was happy with the changes. "I was able to get the whole shop moving again," he says. "I could see that the staff was flourishing. And I knew that they said to themselves: 'Thank God, we have a man up there again who knows what is happening, a guy who has some ideas!' You cannot imagine how much power you unleash with that feeling within a company.

"Of course, I could never have done all that by myself; I could only stimulate and convince my co-workers. Here I come back to the human factor, to leadership. It was an astonishing experience for me, to see how many people were willing to play. It was for this reason that, in such a short time, I could turn the company around and take it to the level of magnitude and to the position that forms the basis of the good work we are able to do today. People know now how to move things ahead."

For Maucher it all boiled down to leadership. "People may or may not admit it, but it makes a huge difference in a company whether the top man is any good or not. The leader is nothing without his people, but all his people together are relatively little without a good man at the helm.

That continues to be the case, despite all the computers and intellectual ideas in the world."

Throughout his career Maucher always preferred a paradoxical strategy of embracing both long-term considerations and the quick response. "It is one of my management principles to be conservative in values, principles, and commitments," says Maucher. "However, with respect to technological and other developments, such as consumer trends, we want to be dynamic and stay in a leadership position. You will hear some people saying about us, 'They are old-fashioned and conservative.' Others, however, will say, 'Damn it, those guys always know what is going on!' Both statements are true. We are not willing to give up precepts that, in my view, have stood the test of time over the last ten thousand years and will outlast the next ten thousand as well. But in other areas, we want to be at the cutting edge of things."

Maucher believes it is essential for a CEO to decide when a corporation must take a leadership position and when it has to tread carefully. "Most managers get mixed up in this respect, or they cannot withstand the pressure, when others approach them with all sorts of ideas," he observes. "They may not have a feeling for what has to be done. For example, many corporations slept through the first few years of the Internet. I see the greatest danger to Nestlé in the possibility that in time the staff will stop asking new questions."

Maucher goes on to say that the boss of any enterprise

has the "damn job" of urging his employees to keep ahead of the curve: "The leader has to have a feeling for what is happening and he constantly has to ask: 'Did you notice that?' 'Have you thought of that?' Once you lose that curiosity, I would almost say obsession, then things are bad. Once the others tell you, 'You did not understand this,' or even worse, when they say, 'We have to be very careful how we break it to him that the world has changed,' then things are truly dreadful. I had done that for years, pulling the others up with me.

"There is only one reason for older people to step down, in my opinion, and that is because some part of them cannot keep up. There are those who are old at thirty-five, old in the head...others still have it at eighty. For this reason I am not in favor of rigid age limits: they are always too early or too late. I would support greater flexibility. But then the criterion really has to be—aside from normal health—whether the person is still with it, is still curious...whether he still feels things."

Sitting opposite Helmut Maucher, you immediately know that he is someone who has not reached his own limits. Although he is seventy-four years old, he seems to be in his late fifties. What one first notices is his intense mental presence. He engages with his conversational partners, listens to their questions, and answers them very specifically. At the same time, he has already started to circle the subject, to fill it out, to find new and different aspects of it. His judgments are quick, but he supports them with good reasons.

Maucher does not like making vague estimates; he

does not speculate about the hidden causes of things. This is reflected in his style of talking. Functional expressions, which can sound a bit like slogans and sometimes sound even a bit crude, allow him to get a grip on his central point. His focus is so sharp that he could sound cutting if his sentences were taken out of context.

For Maucher it is just a small step from the past to the future, from an experience to an emerging opportunity. He has achieved a lot, and he was faster and better than most of those around him. Still, there is a wistful look when he tells you about all that can still be done, when he imagines the things that he will not be a part of. "In a hundred years, that will be completely different," he says.

It comes as no surprise that Maucher credits much of his personal success to reliance on his intuition as a basis for decision making. "I am not sure whether it can be developed or whether you are just born with it," he observes. "It is a feeling for what is really moving in the world.

"I have said that for me intuition is a creative evaluation of information ... Some people may work less with purely quantitative analysis, but they collect information. They have a conversation here, another one there. They read the paper. They are in a position to combine what they take in, and out of their collection of assorted facts arises the vision of the future ...

"No one will be able to manage a large corporation successfully unless he is interested in everything that is happening in the world and is able to perceive his business in the context of the trends that he observes. Sometimes I marvel at how few people are in fact able to do that, and yet I do not see it as anything special. It is nothing like genius; it is a perfectly normal way of thinking and combining."

Maucher believes his intuitive skills were key to Nestlé's decision to make him CEO. "Everyone knows that before I came to Vevey, the firm had virtually become an administrative machine. Weaknesses began to surface. Nestlé was still good, but it was not running well. People were frustrated.

"That is why the Swiss board of directors said: 'Now we need Maucher here in Vevey,' even though it is unlikely that a German was their first choice for running Switzerland's biggest corporation. They could have picked someone else. Another man would also have done a good job of running the firm."

That is perhaps true, but a man like Maucher does not often surface in a large corporation. An example of the former CEO's intuitive prowess was his ability to see the growing commercial potential of bottled water. He had realized very early on, long before most other people, that water would become an important consumer offering. Although Nestlé had already acquired a minor share of Vittel in 1969, this was a move towards diversification rather than part of a clear plan based on an understanding of the importance of water as such. Under Maucher's leadership, water was made into a strategic product group during the nineties. Today, Nestlé owns about 15 percent of the world's mineral water concerns and is the leading bottler.

The reasons for Maucher's commitment to the water business are persuasive:

- Every human being needs at least two liters of water a day, as a normal part of nutrition.
- Water is gaining ground as a preferred beverage in the developed countries. It is favored over soft drinks by the calorie-conscious, and it is becoming a global trend to drink water with meals. Moreover, the use of alcohol has declined, as in most developed countries there is now zero tolerance for drinking and driving.
- Looking at the water supply from a global perspective, it is clear that very few regions can offer water so pure that what comes out of the faucet can be enjoyed as a good drink. For one thing, local water is often chlorinated to control germs; for another, anything in the pipes can change the water's taste, making it less palatable.
- Water is becoming a scarce commodity worldwide, and supplying high-quality water is thus an ever more important service.

Helmut Maucher compares a mineral spring to an oil well: you either own it or you do not. By contrast, you can always build a factory, anywhere. Maucher therefore set himself the task of buying as many sources of high-quality mineral water as possible. With the Perrier Group, Nestlé acquired a whole string of wells. The Italian water company

San Pellegrino also passed completely into Nestlé's hands in 1998.

In the United States, for a long time consumers showed no interest at all in water as a beverage. For this reason Nestlé was able to buy wells there at very reasonable prices. It now owns one-quarter of the entire American mineral water business. With the rate of water consumption rising in North America, Nestlé is now making $1 billion each year through sales of mineral water in the U.S.

Nestlé also owns mineral springs in Mexico, Lebanon, Egypt, China, Vietnam, Poland, Bulgaria, and several other countries. In addition, it exports mineral water brands like Vittel and Valvent.

The prestige brands are what make the most money. If you want to drink a bottle of Perrier in Tokyo—and you might, since it is a status symbol there—you will be paying for a lot more than just the cost of transporting it to Japan!

Good water is increasingly sought after in developing countries as well. Nestlé expects the greatest growth in these regions. At the beginning of 1997, therefore, the corporation took the bold step of entering the area of plain drinking water. The goal was to make available a product with balanced mineral content at a price low enough to be generally affordable.

In April 1997, the Nestlé research center in Lausanne began to create the formula for the composition of the mineral salts and to define the taste profile of the new water. The project was then turned over to Perrier Vittel in France for technical testing. Its mandate was to design a compact production line that could be installed anywhere in the world where a source of acceptable water exists. After the complete purification of the original water, the necessary minerals would be added.

By December 1997 the company was ready to undertake full industrial testing of the water production process, in Ozarka, Texas. Consumer testing began in June 1998 in Pakistan, Thailand, Mexico, and Brazil. In December of that year the new water was placed on the market by Nestlé Pakistan, under the name Nestlé Pure Life. One year later, over fifteen thousand retail outlets had been established. As a result of this phenomenal success, Nestlé Pure Life has since been marketed in Brazil, China, Thailand, Philippines, Mexico and Argentina with other markets soon to follow. In Europe, an equivalent product—a natural spring water originating from various sources—is being marketed under the label Nestlé Aquarel.

Nestlé is also looking at water conservation through technologies that would reduce the amount of water used in manufacturing and agriculture. This research includes the genetic improvement of certain nutritional plants to permit them to survive with less water.

Nestlé's entry into the water market followed an established Maucher formula: "Let us do what is normal and sensible first. Let us produce goods that we can sell, let's pay attention to our management, personnel, and customers. Let us check the till."

Some may wonder what is so remarkable about this

approach. After all, it is common knowledge that all people in charge of large businesses do the same—don't they? It may be common knowledge, but it is often untrue. Look at the computer industry, for example, where massive amounts of money were invested in the development of microchips that no one wants any more. In the food business, thirty thousand new products hit the market annually in Germany alone. Of these, over one-half will have disappeared by the end of the year because they turned out not to be marketable.

Among things normal and sensible, Maucher also counts the sober evaluation of measures to rationalize operations. Putting such measures into action is part of it as well. This means quick structural adjustments to growth and to a changing environment. As CEO he led his staff not to expect corporate support for the preservation of outmoded processes. Instead, he required them to remain flexible and adjust to changing circumstances, both professionally and regionally.

While Maucher's approach was the polar opposite of slash and burn, he was not afraid to make tough decisions. This attitude made him few friends among the staff affected by such decisions, as well as union bosses and shop stewards. Maucher once sold a factory in Karlsruhe that employed 224 people, and he downsized a Maggi production unit in Singen by a third because he felt production costs and wages were too high in that region of Germany. People opposed to these measures cited the company's worldwide earnings, saying, in essence, that a firm that earns so much money can occasionally afford the luxury of operating at a loss.

This argument may make sense to those directly affected by the event, but it is no way to run a company. As Maucher himself says: "A good social climate—yes. A peaceful idyll—no." In these instances he applied a higher criterion for assessing the situation, namely, that the whole is more important than its parts. This does not go against his general management rule that the focus should be on people and products instead of on the system as such. In making those cutbacks, his thinking was long term. He was acting like a leader.

At Nestlé the style of leadership is open and egalitarian—with the important proviso that on every level there is only one boss. Maucher did not believe in collective leadership; he had no confidence in committees. He preferred "a team with a leader" to "a team as the leader." For Maucher the most important requirements for efficient use of human resources and for motivating colleagues were wide control spans, few levels of management, delegation of responsibility, and competence. Maucher had his own view of organizational management.

He still thinks that corporations tend to use systems to replace good leadership. Where no clear leadership exists, personnel systems multiply in the form of salary determination, evaluation, classification, and detailed instructions on how to supervise workers. All this costs a lot of money and generates none. On the contrary, it serves to discourage initiative and may channel human resources in the wrong directions. Maucher believes in reducing personnel functions radically by aligning leadership with what is necessary and what makes sense. This allows managers to perform many personnel functions that grow naturally out of their awareness as leaders.

Maucher kept to an absolute minimum the number of corporation-wide strategies and management rules. He wanted each country, each region, branch, or product group, to create its own rules of conduct. The only area where he insisted on uniformity was with systems and methods that were designed to control recurring processes, for example the manufacture of products.

When it came to personnel, marketing, and product quality, he opted for more flexibility. Anything that depended on consumer preference, local competition, or any other external condition, Maucher left in local hands. His general policy was to align corporate management as far as possible with regional conditions, national mentality, and local events. "It is not our policy to have a large business at home with a few satellites abroad," he stated. "We do not want to be outsiders abroad, we want to be insiders there. Of course, everyone should know what Nestlé is, where Nestlé comes from, and what our basic philosophy is. We bring to all our branches certain Swiss virtues, such as pragmatism, realism, and a positive attitude to work. Everyone should also know that we are open to the world and liberal."

Another central tenet of Maucher's management strategy for Nestlé was the maintenance of a climate of innovation. Anyone who was not willing to innovate or to take the initiative was for Maucher a person who had failed to act—in other words, not an entrepreneur. Maucher did not look for spectacular changes and ideas; he did believe in noticing and appreciating the smallest improvements. Many relatively minor renovations and improvements kept the company's spirit alive.

Occasionally, Maucher resorted to managing by provocation, because sometimes a challenging statement by the boss can most efficiently start the processes of thought and action. To bring about changes, the leader needs power, authority, and credibility. What one says and what one does have to be congruent. For Maucher, personal contact with managers and staff was always of the utmost importance. Because he set a high value on working with the leaders in each country, about half his time was spent abroad. His successor, Peter Brabeck, maintains the same style of managing by traveling about.

The Maucher style of human resources management included an efficient flow of information to and from colleagues and workgroups. Colleagues need to be informed. Information creates security and identification with the company. Direct oral communication in simple, straightforward language is more important than complex descriptions and booklets. Leaders need background information. Co-workers appreciate direct information about their workplace and the things that affect them personally much more than brochures describing in abstract terms the activities and structures of the corporation.

Another area in which Maucher left his stamp was the refinement of Nestlé's external image. The image of an enterprise serves two major purposes for management: first, it becomes the vision that serves as a basis for long-term operations; second, it attracts good leaders and workers, and binds them to the enterprise.

A corporation's image, according to Maucher, is created in the first instance by facts such as size, ranking, earnings, market position, and, above all, products and brands. Image, however, is also a result of the corporate culture. The closer reality is to the image that is projected, the better. Conversely, the farther the image is twisted away from the realities of the corporate culture, the more precarious the long-term future of the business. Because of this understanding, Maucher insisted that the state of Nestlé's business, as well as its actions and products, coincide with public reports about the firm.

"It is really very simple," explains Maucher. "Only when you say what is really the case, especially about things that are unpleasant, do you achieve credibility." Maucher remains certain that economic and social responsibility is becoming more significant with respect to a corporation's image. What matters is what you actually do, not how you talk about it.

As chairman and CEO, Maucher relied totally on the persuasive power of facts. Yet because of this innate bent of his thinking, he did not give enough weight to the emotional power and impact of the critics of Nestlé. He did not understood that rational arguments would not allay the distrust and suspicions of Nestlé that its critics had generated in the public's mind.

Maucher now believes that there is no shortage of information with which to build the image of a large corporation; however, there is a credibility deficit, as he calls it, and current methods of information dissemination cannot completely fill this gap. "Nowadays," he says, "a corporation's image can be very powerfully affected by the media, in either a positive or a negative way. The media, after all, affect not only the various audiences in a corporation's environment; they also reach those within the company. When the media said something about me, the staff read that with much greater interest than any appeals or newsletters that I might address to them directly. I had occasion to call this process 'management by interview.'"

While it is very likely that Maucher's interviews with the press were read and evaluated by his staff in terms of the everyday realities at Nestlé, it is unlikely that Nestlé's critics ever gave Maucher's statements the benefit of a rational evaluation.

So what can an enterprise do when caught in a communications double bind? If information is released, it is said that the corporation is creating a smokescreen to hide the realities. If the firm gives no information, it is said to be concealing the truth. Under such circumstances Maucher sees the job of those entrusted with communications—and that includes top management—as requiring a two-pronged approach. Externally, the aim is to keep the public, including interest groups and critics, informed. The idea here is simply to create awareness and understanding of the company's work. Internally, the task is to keep managers and others aware of possible reactions to the company's economic or entrepreneurial decisions.

While the company's decisions may be correct in themselves, certain groups may perceive them as wrong. Managers have to be prepared to review their decisions, and to decide to make an adjustment or to intensify their efforts to explain their actions. This is why top management has to pay attention to a bi-directional flow of information: it is not easy to delegate the job of handling the reactions of the media and the public.

In Maucher's view it is becoming more and more important for the head of an enterprise to be involved in communications. "We need top managers who are at home with new means of communication. I mean people who have a gift for communication. I am not referring here to the latest technical gadgets. I mean the courage and the calm to talk about company business openly, internally as well as with the outside world."

He also warns of the danger of inflating personality at the expense of the company's image. "The image of the corporation has to have permanence, even if the top man has a plane accident the next day. I do believe that the problem can be solved, if the man who personifies or leads a company remains in harmony with it, so that no breaks can occur."

In other words, from the point of view of the company, it is never about Maucher or Brabeck, but about Nestlé.

A significant aspect of a corporation's image is the way the firm deals with others, and according to Maucher, it matters how you deal not just with your customers but also with your suppliers. Maucher told his staff on many occasions: "Treat your suppliers the way our customers want to be treated by us." The image of a corporation has to be uniformly positive, with customers, suppliers, consumers, governments, unions, and all co-workers.

In some respects the image of a large multinational, which includes many different companies, can never be completely controlled; only those aspects that are common to all parts of the company can be managed. However, certain basic principles of style, management, and common sense can serve as shared guiding values for all the firms in the group. Among these Maucher includes realism, openness in communications, avoidance of exaggeration, and a modicum of modesty, combined with taste and style.

The most basic requirement for the maintenance of common principles is training managers to maintain a sensible balance between their personal ambitions and career goals on the one hand, and the interests of the firm on the other.

4

Continuity Within Change:
Peter Brabeck-Letmathe

IN HIS LAST FEW YEARS AS CEO, Helmut Maucher's greatest worry was finding the right man to succeed him. "Many strong types like me can't do it," he admits. "They make their greatest mistake at the end of their career by putting a weak man in their seat. Some can't even find a successor. Examples of that are all around us."

Maucher admits that it is partly a matter of luck if you can find just the right successor. Admittedly, as soon as he was installed in Vevey, he began to build management and groom them for possible succession. Yet the men he was working with at that time did not seem quite right.

Maucher first got to know Peter Brabeck in Venezuela, when Brabeck was head of the Nestlé company there. Later, Maucher called him to Vevey, first to manage Culinary Products, then as general manager of marketing, and finally as the executive in charge of four of the Strategic Business Units. This gave the two men a chance to work closely together.

Maucher had the growing conviction that Brabeck might be the right man to take his place. "That is why I eventually had a talk with him. That was more than six years ago. I asked, 'What is it you really want to do? Where do you want to go?' And he answered, 'To be honest, at some point, I would like to have your job.' Then I answered, 'OK, you are in the pipeline.' That was our personnel interview."

Brabeck recalls that memorable conversation: "I kept hoping that I would be sent back into the thick of the action. Around the world there were several large, challenging markets that interested me. So I told him that I felt I had done my time in the head office, I wanted to go back out to the front.

"That raised the issue, and it was then that he simply asked me: 'What is it you really want to do?' So I answered quite spontaneously, 'Well, since you ask me, one day I want to sit on the chair which you are occupying now.' At that moment we both felt very good. It was the beginning of a very deep trust, which we have maintained ever since."

Maucher describes how things unfolded after that. "So I pulled him in. I made the decision public about two years ahead of time, so that all rumors would stop. From then on it was official and I could show him everything, so that he was ready when I gave up the job. For a few years I was able to accompany him, as his so-called Active Chairman. He already had 80 percent of the power. Yet he could also come for advice, or in some instances had to do so, according to what we had agreed on. Now [I thought] he is ready, and I am going to disappear.

"On the first day after the shift of power I told him:

'Starting tomorrow morning, your first job now is to train people who will be able to succeed you. It is a long process and it does not always work out. That is the most important thing you will do. In the end it is all done by human beings.'"

Maucher is very open about the fact that, although he felt quite close to all his co-workers, there is a special bond that ties him to Peter Brabeck. Their friendship deepened over the years of their collaboration. But even in this satisfying work relationship Maucher, as the boss, maintained a certain reserve, because it is always possible in a corporation that—in the interest of the firm—decisions will have to be made that could cause emotional problems.

There are two other principles the top person has to follow, in Maucher's opinion, and these are even more important than facing the succession issue itself. One is to train people who can succeed; this is the most important of all. But almost equally important is the duty to play fair at the end, and to go when it is time to go, so as not to spoil the game for the one that comes after.

"It is hardly possible to leave too early," says Maucher. "A good man will become impatient. He will say to himself, 'I won't wait fifteen years till the old man steps down.' Another reason why you cannot stay too long is that the pressure on you mounts and gets very intense towards the end." Maucher's own arrangements for his retirement and succession took four years, without counting the unofficial portion of the process. He thinks that going public at the general shareholders' meeting eighteen months in advance constituted about the right time frame.

Continuity Within Change: Peter Brabeck-Letmathe

Peter Brabeck-Letmathe is Austrian. Born in 1944, he studied business administration and began his professional career with Nestlé in Vienna, selling ice cream for their subsidiary, Findus. Later he held various management positions in South America and Switzerland. Starting in 1981 he was head of Nestlé for the whole of Ecuador, moving into a similar position in Venezuela two years later. In 1987 he moved to the Nestlé headquarters in Vevey, taking over the management of the Culinary Products department.

He was promoted in 1992 to general manager responsible for four of Nestlé's Strategic Business Units, namely, Food, Confectionery, Ice Cream, and Pet Food. Simultaneously, Brabeck was also in charge of marketing and communications, before being officially named Maucher's successor. He took over as CEO in 1997.

For many years Peter Brabeck was an ardent mountain climber. He participated in one of the first Austrian expeditions to the Hindu Kush mountain range. This kind of activity requires a very special personality. Beyond the obvious necessity to be in top physical condition, you need to be able to see ahead and to think before you act. As well, you must know how to minimize risk, be reliable, and be willing to trust the reliability of others. Even today Brabeck likes to take long hikes in the mountains to clear his head and think through problems. He does not raise problems; he solves them. He prefers carefully considered decisions to too much spontaneity.

"Continuity within change" remains the core of

Brabeck's and Nestlé's strategy. After all, while working with Helmut Maucher, Brabeck was jointly responsible for strategic thinking, and during the last years of Maucher's tenure Brabeck helped to shape the company's outlook.

"What I am doing," he says, "is to steer the same course that we had set together, and I try to increase efficiency by perhaps setting the sails a bit differently. The result is a certain degree of acceleration. We have improved on what had already been a very good thing. That was the first part." With these very carefully chosen words Brabeck lets the listener know that something has indeed changed.

The second part, Brabeck says, will be the full use of research and development. This aspect of Nestlé has been restructured over the last twelve years, a process in which Brabeck has been deeply involved. He expects that additional markets and new growth will now come from that quarter. The work of the Nutrition Division—which Brabeck created on his first day as CEO of Nestlé—dovetails with that of Research.

Nutrition as such was not the main concern of the new Nutrition Division. The people there were instructed to concentrate on finding bacteria or molecules that could be introduced into existing Nestlé products. After clinical tests these enriched mainstream products are now being successfully marketed. The best-known product of this kind is LC1, but there are many more, some of which are selling well in South America and Asia, and numerous projects are underway. Nutrition as an enrichment of Nestlé's mainstream products is part of Brabeck's long-term plans.

"When we look at the long run," he says, "I see it as my responsibility to move Nestlé from being a purely agro-alimentary business into a company that truly cares about the wellness of consumers . . . We know that good nutrition is more than swallowing carbohydrates, proteins, or fats. To be well nourished, you need an emotional component. It's obvious that we feel totally different when we enjoy eating a balanced meal than when we cram some food into ourselves any which way."

When Brabeck took over from Maucher in 1997, he framed four priorities for his work:

- Innovation and renovation
- Efficient operation
- Greater accessibility of Nestlé products, according to the axiom "Whenever, Wherever, However"
- Better communication with consumers

Brabeck emphasizes that in order to change the complex realities of global markets, the ideas and co-operation of many different people are needed. The leadership of an organization can set realistic yet challenging goals, and it can create the organizational conditions that will align everyone behind these goals. Thus the entire staff can be involved in the creation of concepts and practical solutions. Constant change means that many scenarios will have to be taken into account, while the most pragmatic solutions and the overall goals for the coming years still have to be kept in mind. At any given moment, in other words, one has to work with the knowledge currently available and not spend too much time dreaming about what will happen when new knowledge emerges.

As a means of increasing efficiency, for example, Brabeck uses internal and external benchmarks, which are intended to lead to a better use of available resources. The most efficient components of the global Nestlé Group—be they factories, distribution and administrative centers, or structures—serve as standards for improvement elsewhere, as do the best of Nestlé's global and local competitors.

Brabeck's efforts have already produced clear results. The total cost of all processes related to manufacturing products has gradually been lowered. In 1996 the "cost of products sold" constituted 51.8 percent of their total sales price; in 1997 this dropped to 51.2 percent, and it was even further reduced in 1999, from 50.1 percent to 48.1 percent. In 2001, at the end of this program, this cost accounted to 44.5 percent of sales. "This trend gives us the necessary space to make further improvements in marketing, advertising, and selling. This will allow us to make more gains and achieve more growth."

Brabeck is careful to dispel the notion that this is entirely an initiative from headquarters. "On the contrary," he says, "our structure and organizational culture ensures that our operational components will react with practical suggestions to further any of our general goals. For example, before 1999, our various branches had already achieved a total reduction in our overall costs of 2.2 billion

Swiss francs [U.S. $1.3 billion], and they did it all entirely on their own initiative."

Increasing the efficiency of an industrial outfit involves a combination of cost-saving technologies and shifts in production. Certain products are now made in only a few factories, which supply whole regions. Brabeck adds that certain other, less central production processes have been shifted to third parties. It is a matter of many small improvements here and there, but in a corporation with so many parts these little changes have a large cumulative effect and bring about significant overall improvements.

Of all the changes, the most significant were related to raw materials and to the optimization of various processes. Making full use of the capacity of plants, improving their efficiency, and minimizing losses in the production process were all central considerations.

Brabeck is also reducing the number of production facilities. In 1999 Nestlé either announced or carried out the final shutdown or sale of fifty-four factories. The sale of Findus alone accounted for fourteen of these. In the business year 2000 the total number of factories owned by Nestlé was reduced by thirty, to 479 and to 468 in 2001 (excluding that 29 factories of Ralston Purina acquired at the end of the year). This was made possible in part by the rationalization of production and in part by sales. "We are in the happy position to be able to foresee and plan for these changes," Brabeck says, "and can do them without terminating large numbers of workers. We will continue to pursue this policy in the future.

"We regard the reconstruction of Nestlé as part of our daily operations. That is also the reason why we at Nestlé account for the costs of our restructuring before we calculate the final results of our operations for the year. Annual restructuring costs run to 300 or 400 million Swiss francs [$178–238 million]. Our policy of continual improvement offers fewer opportunities to financial speculators; for us, it is a way to live up to our responsibilities to the community."

For Brabeck, restructuring includes selling off various business activities that are of little strategic significance and that do not promise satisfactory levels of long-term profitability. Processes that can be carried out more efficiently by specialized businesses are another group of activities that is being sold, as long as results still meet Nestlé's quality standards. One example is the processing of cocoa, which can be done very well by specialists in Malaysia and Italy. All in all, the 1999 cleanup of Nestlé's portfolio netted more than $1 billion.

It is one of Brabeck's main concerns that lowering costs should not involve lowering the quality of Nestlé products. Global presence for Nestlé means maintaining its claim to the highest quality in certain salient areas. These key areas, clearly defined by the central leadership, represent the Nestlé Group's core competencies. It is in these areas that all units concentrate their developmental efforts, in order to keep their technological edge and retain their leadership with respect to quality.

Core competence means a lot more to Brabeck than just having superior knowledge about certain processes and products, their composition and special properties. Building competence in any key sector of the global food market takes ten to fifteen years of steady work, and can cost between $300 million and $600 million in research and development.

Ensuring the accessibility of products is part of any effective marketing concept. This speaks directly to Brabeck's third priority of "Whenever, Wherever, However." Simply stated, this means that for a product to have a better presence, it must be available no matter when, where, or how the consumer happens to want it.

Delivering on this promise is a multi-faceted process, which begins with the appearance and packaging of the product. Take the example of a product like Nesquik, a powdered chocolate drink that was originally designed to be prepared and consumed at home. Since, as a powder, it cannot be consumed on the spot, Nesquik also had to be made available in liquid form. As well, in order to follow the single consumer home or to the office, this beverage also has to be offered in small packages that contain a few convenient single servings, ready to be mixed.

The same goes for Nescafé, which is available in liquid form in Germany under the name Café Viennois, for those who want to enjoy it away from home, as well as in little serving-size bags, for traditional use. The small packages are convenient to carry and also cater to people who can afford to buy only a few at a time.

Accessibility does have its limits, and Nestlé

understands where its expertise stops. Brabeck is certain, for example, that Nestlé will never go into the retail business. Conversely, he believes that most retailers who used to think they should produce their own foods are coming around to a complementary view, namely, that it is better and cheaper to leave production to those who specialize in it.

"We have now reached the point where everyone at Nestlé understands his core competence," Brabeck says with satisfaction. In emerging countries this means that the corporation works with local wholesalers to bring its products to consumers more cheaply and efficiently than they were able to do under older distribution systems. Traditionally, in emerging countries, the system for the distribution of goods involved several levels of wholesalers who moved goods down to the local level. The chain could be pretty long, as goods were handed from one level to the next, and as each trading level added its margin, the price of the product rose steadily. Nestlé now distributes its goods directly to levels that are nearer to the consumer. As a result there are only a few wholesalers in the distribution chain, although sub-wholesalers for local markets still exist.

Brabeck believes that globalization of commerce, which brings with it modern logistical systems, is to the advantage of local consumers. Since a lower price can mean more sales, the new systems will also profit Nestlé.

This strategy applies to industrialized countries as well, where large shippers and retailers serve very different consumer demands from those in the developing economies.

In America, Europe, Australia, and Japan, talking about the "mass consumer" makes less and less sense in an increasingly segmented market. "When I look at the elaborate segmentation...it is obvious to me that there is no such thing as the 'mass consumer,'" says Brabeck.

Consumers in the industrialized countries are also buying more goods through new distribution channels, and this is true especially of foods and beverages. Brabeck cites one example to explain this point. At one time you had to go to the supermarket to buy pet food. Today, in contrast, there are specialized pet food centers, and you can also find pet food at garden centers, at the veterinarian's, and in highly specialized animal supply stores. "The last few years have seen immense segmentation [in this sector] and very high growth rates," notes Brabeck. "In the beverage sector, growth has been far greater for out-of-home consumption than for in-home use."

The "Whenever, Wherever, However" policy has other aspects as well. Different departments at Nestlé deal with prices, discounts, the design of promotions, strategy around various distribution channels, and sales organizations. "It is not enough any more for our products to stand neatly on the supermarket shelves. They have to be in all sorts of retail channels, from the small corner store, to the cart of the street vendor, all the way to the Internet. All this has contributed to making the full accessibility of our products into a very complex challenge."

In the United States today, half of all the food eaten is consumed outside the home. Nestlé developed its FoodServices sector years ago, and it is now bringing in more than $3.5 billion annually. The realm of FoodServices offers various food products and drinks for wholesale customers, and this sector's annual growth rate of 5.3 percent is well above the Nestlé Group's average. The reason for this is that, in addition to the classic outlets in the area of food preparation—the fast-food chains, restaurants, cafeterias, and so on—new distribution channels are gaining in importance. Thus Nestlé has signed a contract with the Esso gasoline stations in Latin America that makes it possible to open a Nescafé coffee bar at any of their stations.

In Japan, another channel was opened through the purchase from Ueshima of 100,000 automatic beverage dispensers. "In that country, literally thousands of people stand in front of automats in the streets," says Brabeck. "We were determined to expand the market for our ready-to-drink coffee and tea."

Nestlé had already entered the Japanese beverage-dispensing business some ten years ago, through a joint venture with Otsuke. By 1999, Nestlé had gained 4 percent of that market. Its market share will double, according to Brabeck's plans, with the recent addition of 300,000 more automats.

The Internet represents for Brabeck another very important new distribution channel. Back in the early nineties Nestlé was already facing the challenge of this new medium: it was the first food producer to try marketing on the Net. At that time the corporation introduced "Nestlé

Easy Shop" as a test. Later it became a co-founder of the first Internet Shop in Switzerland. At first it was purely a matter of gaining some experience and finding out to what extent this new market would require changes in the range of products, in packaging, and so on.

Since then Nestlé in the U.S.A. has signed agreements with a large number of Internet firms, such as WebPan, Peapod, Homegrocer, Netgrocer, Shoplink, etc. Nestlé has also created an operational structure to deal exclusively with this new distribution channel. In short, the matter is given high priority.

Nestlé does not intend to become involved in the physical distribution of its products. Brabeck wants to leave that part of the business to the experts, to wholesale distributors like Tesco. This corporation is already the largest "e-tailer" in the world, and counts itself among those internationally active business partners with whom Nestlé has built a very good working relationship.

That said, Brabeck does not consider an expression such as "the New Economy" to be very apt: "There is an economy of things and there is an economy of information. I find this division makes more sense." Yet without question, the intangible economy has had a great impact on the food industry, and especially on the way a company of Nestlé's magnitude now has to be run.

The company's current aim is to improve the technological aspects of its food delivery on the one hand and its food production on the other. Brabeck is certain that state-of-the-art technology will improve security and reliability in the economy of things, that is, with respect to the delivery of food to the customer. This is an indispensable prerequisite if the economy of information is to continue to attract the public with its simplicity and efficiency.

On the food production end, Brabeck says "the economy of information will help improve the logistics of industry and commerce. We will, nonetheless, continue to use knife and fork and to put something real into our mouths…In the food industry, the economy of things is and always will be the most important component."

Innovation and renovation (the renewal of existing products) is Peter Brabeck's third priority. Nestlé's annual R & D expenses are now about $690 million. Their purpose is to improve the competitive edge of Nestlé products rather than launch the "next big thing." "In many cases it is a mistake to wait for the grand technological breakthrough," says Brabeck. "Many small improvements will often produce better results."

Innovations based on research and development, Brabeck says, require clear vision and a long-term strategy. Biotechnology is a good example. Basic research in this area began in the early eighties. Nestlé wanted to form its own judgment about this new field, in order to be able to guarantee the safety of its customers right from the start. After achieving some very positive results, Nestlé is now turning to practical applications of this new technology, which have already become reality in many parts of the world.

"In terms of this technology," notes Brabeck, "certain

developing countries, like Brazil and Ecuador, are much farther advanced than Europe. China is even assuming a leading role in the development and the applications of biotechnology."

Brabeck's positive attitude to gene technology is not affected by its negative reception on the part of consumers in various countries. Within the last year alone, 12 million hectares of land have been planted with genetically improved crops in the United States, Canada, and Argentina—mostly soybeans, corn, and canola. This obviated the need for several million liters of pesticides. In Brabeck's opinion, friends of the environment should enthusiastically welcome this kind of positive result from new technology, "but this is unfortunately not yet the case."

As a global enterprise, Nestlé has a global responsibility. Together with other leading members of the industry, Nestlé will continue to make every effort to communicate openly and clearly with consumers, with the aim of convincing them of the advantages of biotechnology.

Brand names and effective communication constitute the fourth key priority for Nestlé. At present the Nestlé Group invests billions in the media alone; total marketing costs run to more than 15 percent of sales—reason enough to merit the attention of top leadership.

The main goals of consumer communications for Brabeck continue to be image, credibility, and the integrity of the enterprise. Since media have become international in scope, their significance has increased for multinationals that market name brands. Media communications, with its global dimensions, is replacing glossy brochures.

Brabeck fully understands that in order to anchor Nestlé positively and securely in the perception of its customers and of the general public, the values and principles of the corporation must be upheld—he uses the word "lived"—as a consistent and long-term commitment. Only this consistency will ensure the credibility of its managers and of the corporation's stand on issues.

One such issue is Nestlé's commitment to improve the quality of life through its global presence. "It is our principle that the investments we make in any region should also benefit the country where we are investing," says Brabeck. "First of all, local distributors and the local economy in general should profit from the value Nestlé is creating. On one level the activities of a multinational tend to impart information and know-how to local suppliers. These could be the farmers who deliver their milk or coffee beans to the factory, or the firms that manufacture the packaging materials we use.

"Nestlé is interested in building long-term partnerships. For this reason it is the corporation's policy to refrain from making opportunistic, short-term gains by depressing prices. In the medium and long term, of course, prices have to adjust to the conditions of the general market, in order for Nestlé to remain competitive."

Brabeck's words are finding a receptive audience in the Third World, as more countries there open themselves to the rest of the world. They are deregulating, modernizing, and globalizing their economies. This means that as they remove obstacles, they are enjoying a greater share of the wealth that is created globally. It often happens that the so-called developing countries turn out to be freer in their thinking, more "global," than the industrialized countries. This is true, for example, with respect to telecommunications or when a country establishes internationally accepted and standardized accounting practices.

Brabeck is convinced that great benefits accrue to a country from free competition and the unrestricted merging of international and local capital. In his opinion this works better than forcing the local economy to operate on the basis of decisions made by the government.

Brabeck is here addressing a major issue: do multinationals create permanent prosperity, or do they merely relocate their operations, from one country or continent to another, as it suits their corporate objectives? For Brabeck the answer is clear: global enterprises, and especially worldwide food producers like Nestlé, maintain a worldwide network, filled with ideas, brand names, guarantees, and human capital. They establish direct and indirect connections to institutions, enterprises, and local governments. They are integrated into the local economy as well as into a network of global economic relations. Above all, they are in the business of creating value wherever they operate.

5

Nestlé:

A Long-Term Investment

ESTLÉ HAS NO MAJOR shareholder who could
possibly pursue special interests or interfere sin-
gle-handedly in the management of the corporation. Nestlé shares are widely scattered, in the hands of
more than 200,000 shareholders. More than half of the
shares are held by institutional investors, such as pension
funds, trusts, and insurance companies. More and more
employees are also buying shares of their company.

The majority of Nestlé stock is held in Europe. Of the
shareholders, 53 percent are Swiss, 13 percent are French, 8
percent German, and 6 percent British. Only 12 percent of
Nestlé's shares are in the United States, and another 8 percent in other countries, outside Europe. Nestlé shares are
traded on the stock exchanges of Zurich, Frankfurt,
London, and Paris. American Depositary Receipts (ADRs)
based on Nestlé shares can be purchased in the United
States.

The wide distribution of the corporation's shares has
the advantage of allowing the management to act

independently. When one person or group owns a large block of shares of a corporation, it is always a possibility that such a major stockholder will want to interfere in the operations of the corporation in pursuit of his or her own ends. To prevent this, Nestlé has instituted a bylaw that forbids any one person or agency from wielding more than 3 percent of the voting power at the general shareholders' meeting; nor is there any shareholder known to hold more than 3 percent of the capital. At any rate, the value of the share capital has by now reached such magnitude that hardly anyone could afford a so-called hostile takeover of Nestlé.

At Nestlé, shareholder value means mostly long-term growth. The fundamental management principles laid down for Nestlé are outlined below.

In the interest of its shareholders, Nestlé wants to increase value. Yet the corporation does not seek to maximize short-term profits and share value at the expense of the successful long-term development of the enterprise. At the same time, Nestlé is always conscious of the necessity to achieve respectable profits every year.

"No one is blind to the actual realities and demands of financial markets," says Brabeck. "Yet in the interest of our private and institutional investors, we focus on harmonizing the short-term challenges of the financial markets with long-term profitability and growth targets."

It has been said that the economy has become inhuman because everything seems to be sacrificed for short-term profit. Brabeck's answer: "How long could the top management of an enterprise afford the luxury of ignoring the complaints of consumers, suppliers, employees, and governmental agencies, simply in order to give their shareholders good profits? In the long view—and that is Nestlé's view—only those enterprises will reach their goals that are able to walk the knife edge between the opposing demands made on them."

For Maucher, too, a fundamental misunderstanding of enduring values and investments is at the root of many current managerial mistakes. "This is where we are lacking most, nowadays ... We have people romping about, some of them barely twenty-five, who have never seen a factory from the inside. They analyze balance sheets and offer us fantastic ideas on what all we should do [to maximize short-term value].

"Many of these clowns would like to play yo-yo with us, because at year-end each of them has to show that the performance of his stack of papers outdoes that of his colleagues by a few fractions of a percentage. This is what leads to this short-sighted maximizing and optimizing within the capital markets. Yet at the same time, industrial processes and the investment decisions connected with them tend to become more and more long-range ... Some enterprises have granted their financial people too much power; now they are completely in the hands of these investment types. This is a source of real danger for the companies in question, and for capitalism itself.

"If you think long-term, you also pay much closer attention to the image of the enterprise. I have in mind things like ethics, like the environment, investing in research, and perspectives that will motivate the employees, such as long-term training and development of staff. All of this is vitally important to the future of the company, but none of these points will bring in any profit in the next three months.

"There is a tendency today, which some industrial leaders follow, to destroy the corporation in the long run, only to maximize their short-term profits. I have had to battle such people too. But long-term investors are re-emerging—good people, who can see the point of long-range investments and who are willing to walk all the way with their chosen corporations.

"Many enterprises do not make any more acquisitions because they say that they do not want to water down their short-term gains and send their shares diving. Their financial analyst would spank them, you see. They are not willing to bear that, even though it would have been the correct thing to do in the long run."

Brabeck adds that in all the current talk about shareholder value, what is often overlooked is that satisfied, loyal customers constitute the most stable basis for the value of an economic enterprise. "In the food business, well-presented brand names are the means and the value in one. For an enterprise like Nestlé, they are more valuable than buildings and machinery."

The following figures show that Nestlé's efforts to augment long-term value have been successful: The market value of all Nestlé shares listed rose from $14 billion to $33.5 billion between 1987 and 1997. At the end of 2001 this figure had reached $81.6 billion. This represents more than a sixfold growth from 1987 to the present. The dividend has grown from $12 to $38.10 (in reality 3.81, due to the share split which occured in 2001) since 1990.

The shares of food manufacturers are generally considered crisis-safe. After all, people will always eat and drink, and the population is ever increasing. Nonetheless, in 1999 on the stock exchanges of the world, the shares of this sector tended to be neglected. Whereas that year the index of all shares traded on Wall Street went up by 23 percent, the Dow Jones Index for food and beverages dropped by 14 percent. The large food corporations could not hold their share prices steady, and by the end of the year they had all lost share value—except Nestlé. By year-end 1999 the price of Nestlé shares had increased 4 percent since January 1 of that year. In contrast, Danone dropped by 7 percent, Sara Lee by 21.5 percent, H.J. Heinz by 30 percent, Unilever by 24.5 percent, and Philip Morris by a whopping 55 percent.

There are several reasons why investors had come to neglect the stocks of multinational food corporations. The decline in consumer spending in Europe was one reason. Another is that food manufacturers have to rely on retailers, and many of these had been ousted from markets everywhere. There were the economic crises in Asia, Latin America, and Russia. And on top of all that came the trend on exchanges everywhere to align with high-tech values, especially information technology, where quick gains could be expected.

Since then, more and more banks have placed food industry shares back on their lists of recommended investments. They argue that good gains are still possible, because the general trend, in the wake of the implosion of the dot.com stocks, is beginning to shift back to more conservative investing.

Financial analysts agree that the stocks of food corporations with a strong commitment to emerging markets have the most to gain. That is where enormous growth will take place, and Nestlé is way ahead of its competitors in that area: presently, the corporation makes one-third of its sales in countries with emerging economies.

Unlike its competitors, Nestlé did not pull back from these areas during the Asian economic crisis. While other food corporations contracted their activities for short-term reasons, Nestlé used this time to build up its market share. Because of the company's foresight, analysts are always more willing to recommend Nestlé than any of its competitors. They also appreciate that Nestlé has been working on its restructuring for a long time, and that the first fruits of that process were discernible in the numbers for the 1999 business year. Some of Nestlé's competitors, meanwhile, are just beginning to restructure.

6

Leaders, Not Systems:
The Nestlé Way

"I F YOU TREAT PEOPLE AS YOU find them, you will make them worse; if you treat them as they could be, you will make them better."

This quotation from Goethe, one of Helmut Maucher's favorites, encapsulates Nestlé's philosophy about its employees. It is also one of the linchpins of "Basic Management and Leadership Principles at Nestlé," a brochure Maucher and Brabeck wrote in 1997, when the latter took over the position of CEO. At that time it was distributed worldwide, in all branches of Nestlé.

For Maucher the quotation precisely defines the art of leadership: "One talent is always important to me: the ability to lead. That means developing people's potential and motivating people. It happens again and again that these matters are not allotted the attention they deserve, often because of time constraints. This is strange, because anyone ought to see that this is important, since everything happens through people. When you have the right people they will do the right thing."

A sharp focus on people, co-workers, and leadership is in his view a decisive, if not *the* decisive, factor in long-term success. Not that Maucher is unaware of the need for and the value of systems within complex organizations. His point is that at Nestlé such systems must remain aids to leadership and to operations, and never become ends in themselves. Great importance is attached to the training and personal development of staff, and to the corporation's relationship with workers. What really counts at Nestlé are attitudes, the general atmosphere in the workplace, a direct and personal leadership style, the credibility of leaders, and how they deal with workers—and that includes relations across national and cultural boundaries and between corporate branches.

What all this means is often revealed incidentally. A secretary, who only rarely had contact with Maucher, was surprised to find that he knew her by name and even remembered to inquire after the health of her husband, who had been severely ill for a long time. She would never have expected the head of the company to notice or remember such details.

The close connection between Nestlé employees is evident whenever two of them meet for the first time. They will already have heard of each other, and will have common Nestlé friends or colleagues. They are likely to know who held the other person's position in the past and built the groundwork for their own work. Many people are in close contact across the world, without ever having met face to face.

Maucher insists that leaders should always assume that

people could do better. This attitude creates trust and allows the staff some latitude. Naturally, Maucher also demands that employees use this freedom in a responsible way; and to act responsibly, one needs a clear idea of the overall goals of the corporation. This approach was Maucher's way of ensuring that Nestlé's leadership would be able to deal with the extreme decentralization of the corporation.

This philosophy does not obviate the need for performance, especially given the way the corporate world is changing. Deploying the right people in the right places has become a more urgent priority, according to Maucher: "I recently told Peter Brabeck that I would not object if he decided to make changes in leadership positions at a speed that is more consistent with the current pace of business. We used to be able to wait two, three years. The world moved more slowly then, and we tended to make decisions too late... It is a humane and decent thing to be loyal to a colleague whom you have come to like. You hesitate to move him. [Brabeck] does this faster than I used to, and he has to: times have changed.

"More than before, today every leader has to ask himself daily: How am I going to steer this ship? How do I have to adjust my course, or even the crew and the very shape of my vessel? What has become obsolete? You cannot avoid it. To be able to make these changes rationally and in time, without losing one's humanity: that is the hardest balancing act."

Balance is also a factor in the deliberately international composition of management teams, not just at head office but also in Nestlé's foreign branches. At the same time there is an emphasis on identifying local leaders and developing them. This combination ensures more experience and variety in leadership at every level.

At the hub in Vevey, Switzerland, 1,600 people from 60 different countries work together. Brabeck himself is Austrian, and of the nine executive vice presidents, two are American, one Mexican, one Australian, one Spanish, one Swedish, one Dutch and two have dual citizenship.

In choosing potential leaders, Nestlé takes into account education and experience, but the most important criterion is personality. The qualities they look for include strength of character, a sense of responsibility, moral strength, plus more unusual virtues, such as courage, calm, the ability to learn, sensitivity to change, and imagination in visualizing the future. Nestlé also wants people who can encourage a climate of innovation in the workplace, who can perceive connections, and who have credibility. Finally, leaders at Nestlé need to feel international, and they need to be willing to change.

With respect to the latter, job rotation has become a necessary part of management. It provides varied training and development for all leaders, and infuses new ideas into management teams. Equally important in Maucher's view, however, is a full appreciation of continuity in leadership, and of the experience and knowledge acquired on certain long assignments. At Nestlé, the way to ensure the best leadership for the long run is to give some managers long-term jobs, especially within the larger markets; then, after a stint of ten or fifteen years, the manager is ready to take over the top leadership position in that area of the world.

Since Maucher's day Nestlé has also insisted that, in any takeover, there be a good fit between the cultures of the two corporations. Effective integration depends in large part upon the willingness of the leaders of the company that was bought out to accept the changed circumstances. Maucher always tried to avoid hostile takeovers, that is, buying a company whose leadership initially rejects the deal. Bringing an angry management around is a difficult and long-drawn-out process.

It is a venerable Nestlé tradition to emphasize training: every employee should have a chance to prove and develop his or her natural talent, desire to learn, and intention to grow. This opens to every person the chance to work eventually at optimum level. This also means that all employees, irrespective of nationality, can strive for the highest positions if they have the necessary abilities and experience.

To fulfill such ambitious training objectives, the company has to proceed systematically, continuously, and cooperatively. And such a training plan must be viewed as no less important than a good research and development initiative. A corporation now needs an overall, standardized plan for training and also for specialized advanced training. Today, training has to address many issues: the constant progress of science, technological developments, changes in the world economy, the ensuing adjustments in the structure of the corporation, and the increasing diversification of its activities.

At head office in Vevey and at all its branches in Switzerland and abroad, Nestlé distinguishes between training for new employees and advanced courses designed to develop leaders. New employees participate in introductory courses that are selected to fit their exact requirements. Equipped with the information they need to function, many workers then embark on a one- or two-year practicum. Men and women who need more general education might attend appropriate classes. Personal development is also available for experienced employees. They might, for example, study team building or unit management, or choose to update old knowledge in special refresher courses.

One of the principles Maucher propounded to his co-workers was never to remain content with what they knew, but always to strive to learn more. In this spirit, in 1989 he embarked on a major renovation of the Nestlé training center, which had been set up in 1963. Since then, every year, about two thousand Nestlé managers from around the globe complete one- or two-week seminars there. This center is the model for the training centers that have been established in various foreign markets, and it ensures that training for the entire Nestlé Group is uniform.

Nestlé wants to do more than just offer professional advancement to exceptional men and women. It also wants them to absorb the Nestlé culture, the special atmosphere and way of thinking that is the Nestlé style. The Vevey training center doesn't just teach marketing or procedural techniques. At this school, young leaders from around the world can meet and get to know the management staff of the central office. Directors and specialists teach or lead seminars. They also give talks and take part in events outside the formal curriculum.

By making personal connections with students, the leaders make sure that course participants form a clear picture of Nestlé headquarters and of the corporation's leadership, as well as of the responsibilities that the leaders assume. Last but not least, during their course of study, Nestlé employees from all over have a chance to mingle and exchange experiences.

Of course, individual schooling still plays an important role. Practical coaching from one's immediate supervisor retains immense value for the company, and is carried out via work programs, special projects, and, especially, relocations. It is mandatory for an international concern that the leadership at headquarters is able to move into outlying markets, and vice versa.

Nestlé is aware that leadership personnel cannot be developed in a few days, but a good selection of colleagues with appropriate qualifications can support and expand the talents of less experienced staff members. This is also an essential component of planning for the eventual replacement of the leadership team's key members. Maucher always tried to fill leadership positions by internal rather than external recruiting, and this continues to be the Nestlé way. Such a strategy not only creates a degree of internal unity but also allows for timely succession.

Brabeck sees the Vevey training center and other initiatives as part and parcel of Nestlé's commitment to continuous learning. "What you learn today at university will be completely outdated in six years' time," he notes. "However, it is even more important that the people from all over the world meet our top management, that they become steeped in Nestlé culture, familiar with the Nestlé style. For this, we are willing to go to great lengths. I would like to make personal visits to every one of our seminars, to talk with our employees, to discuss things with them. On the whole, I manage to do that pretty regularly."

Brabeck also believes it is crucial that every Nestlé worker acquire a measure of healthy business sense. And in a society based on information, where the total amount of available data doubles about every five years, it matters little what a person has learned in the past. What matters is that he or she is willing to continue to learn in the future.

All of this will have an impact on how the company chooses its leaders. "Nestlé is ready to rise to the challenge," says Peter Brabeck. "I believe we are well prepared because we have become used to changes from working in our own business environment." He is certain that there are no more sacred cows at Nestlé. This is true, he says, not just for products and brand names but also for personnel. In the area of human resources, just as everywhere else, it is necessary to give up beloved old habits and to start questioning things that used to be taken for granted.

Every aspect of personnel work will be affected by change. This applies to hiring new people, promotions, and compensation as much as to the organization of the flow of work and to hierarchical levels. Greater flexibility will allow impatient young people to advance more rapidly, and will make possible better matches between personal preferences and talents on the one hand, and the needs of the organization on the other. Such flexibility will improve the quality of the staff by, for example, allowing more women to gain leadership positions at Nestlé.

The latter touches on a sensitive point for Nestlé, because despite several attempts, up to now the corporation has not succeeded in grooming any women for top leadership positions. One reason for this failure could be that several of the women chosen as potential leaders joined the corporation in mid-career. This made their rise to power more difficult, because a person who joins Nestlé later in life is at a natural disadvantage. The fact is, the rules that govern advancement and the internal competition for the top jobs at Nestlé are substantially different than elsewhere, and the subtleties that ultimately matter may not be easily picked up by relative newcomers.

Brabeck's strategy promises to have a significant impact on Nestlé's future leadership. Currently, almost all members of the senior management in Switzerland have spent their entire professional lives with the corporation. Most of them were market heads in their respective home countries before they went to Vevey.

This type of continuity is completely typical of Nestlé, and by no means limited to its top management. Lifelong careers are still the rule at the corporation. Brabeck makes it very clear, however, that in twenty years this kind of career will be the exception. He foresees the end of the Nestlé tradition that an employee starts with Nestlé at the time of his or her apprenticeship or immediately after graduation and continues with the company until retirement. "We live in a rapidly changing world," he notes. "Even a company with as powerful and tradition-conscious a culture as Nestlé will not be immune to that for ever."

Increasingly, the speed of trade is becoming the main criterion of efficiency. This applies not just to products but also to human beings. The principle of "just-in-time," which is now very familiar in the supply chain, will in future be applied to recruiting human resources as well. Certain specific skills and abilities will be needed at particular points in time, according to Brabeck. The labor market will also become more flexible. This means a permanent willingness and ability to adjust, on the part of both individuals and organizations.

Brabeck also sees the traditional models for employment and hierarchy changing. The line between employment and independent work will become blurred, as many professionals move repeatedly from one employer to the next, now as employees, now on contractual terms. A flexible compensation system will be very important in this scenario, and it will be easier to accept as well.

"In this struggle for talent, smaller employers are slowly but surely beginning to offer significant competition to the large concerns," says Brabeck. "At this time, Nestlé always has more job applicants than we could possibly employ. I do not see this trend as guaranteed for the future, however. We may well end up fighting to win the best talent on the market. The candidates of tomorrow will be more demanding than those of today. The young graduates that enter the job market today are not used to vertical structures. The conditions they demand are often easier to meet in a small organization than in a huge one."

Lean organizational structures, which, according to Brabeck, have become indispensable from a purely cost-saving point of view, also have the advantage of being able to maintain an ambiance that is attractive to entrepreneurial types. Young, talented professionals are more and more in demand, while the workforce as a whole is getting older.

Traditional hierarchical patterns are also undergoing change; it is no longer enough just to be the boss, to have authority. People who are true leaders are recognized for their talent and experience in balancing and harmonizing many abilities and points of view in a team. They know how to set goals that all concerned are willing to work towards. That does not mean that from now on the team will make all decisions; it does mean that a new kind of leadership is emerging. It is that kind of leadership Nestlé intends to nurture.

INSPIRATION OUT OF THE SNOQUALMIE VALLEY

Nestlé's training initiatives are not confined to Europe. Consider the training center in the Snoqualmie Valley, to the west of Seattle. The land was purchased in 1909 by Elbridge Amos Stuart, the founder of the Carnation Company. He was looking to buy a farm for the firm, so that he could raise milk cows. He happened to be on the east coast when the telegram sent by his partner reached him, saying that a suitable farm had been located. Stuart bought it sight unseen—something he would never have done had he inspected the property. It took many years of hard work to turn the place into the model farm that visitors are shown today.

Eventually, the property became a research farm, where some of the world's best milk cows are now bred. It also houses the very first kennels and research labs ever dedicated to the development of dog food—and, later, cat food. All this, as well as a museum and the famous historical rose garden, is open to all Nestlé staff and to the public.

The training center itself is elsewhere on the grounds, near the founder's house and a guest complex. The Stuart mansion offers a gracious, old-fashioned ambiance in which Nestlé executives can meet and exchange views. The events staged in this retreat atmosphere, far from the hectic activities of daily business routines, are meant to allow managers to get to know one another and to explore new ideas.

Much of the training is targeted at what Nestlé USA terms as "high potentials"—people who are part of the company's succession plan. These could range anywhere from managers to senior vice-presidents. The types of training also vary. There are "workout sessions," numbering seven to nine a year where specific functional groups meet to examine a particular topic. One example would be a manufacturing team getting together to discuss "The factory of the future." A second type is international training sessions developed in Vevey that are taught around the world. One or two of these take place every year at the Snoqualmie Valley site with participants from both North and South America. The third type of training is "Nestlé University courses" focusing especially on what the company calls leader development—from leadership basics to strategic business leadership.

In addition the company uses the center for off-site meetings for different teams—say a finance group in which people would examine their department and look for ways to improve it. In addition, Nestlé USA holds two leadership forums annually, which involve 230 of their top people in training sessions lasting almost a week.

All of this training allows for team-building—"quality time together" is how one participant describes it. An added plus is the heritage of the site. "It is," says Claudia Horty, vice-president training and development, "a wonderful place to bring newer employees because they can get a feel for the company."

7

Decentralization: Getting Close to the Markets

"HERE IN SWITZERLAND," says Helmut Maucher, "we have—in addition to the offices and factories of Nestlé Switzerland—our international headquarters, those of the Nestlé SA; but despite all that power, we do not imagine that this is the navel of the world."

This decentralized attitude creates operational strength and flexibility, and it can lead to measures and decisions that are well tailored to the needs of each of the foreign countries involved. This international policy generates motivation and identification with the business among both managers and workers. Decentralization also means, of course, that much more attention has to be paid to the staffing of various workgroups.

With respect to human relations, the organizational structure is as simple as possible, with the fewest possible hierarchical levels. This means wider control spans for all managers. Combined with the corporation's policy of personal attention to its leadership and employees everywhere, these measures make for great flexibility and maintain a generally high level of job satisfaction.

Nestlé is unusually decentralized. Decisions are generally made on the plane where they will be implemented, that is to say, within the markets affected. This does not have any deleterious effects on the efficiency of either the regional or the global administration. Within the overall strategic framework of the corporation, local branches have autonomy, which gives them the needed flexibility to respond to local market conditions.

At the "Center," as Nestlé calls the international headquarters, leadership takes responsibility only for the following matters:

- important strategic decisions and fundamental policy
- essential financial affairs, including significant investment decisions and how to finance them
- general guidelines concerning brand names
- establishment and administration of quality control systems for products
- development of international leadership personnel
- co-ordination between the various markets in the areas of production, imports, and exports
- technical support, delivered by means of a highly developed network that is accessible to all the branches of Nestlé. This includes experts and a large body of specific know-how, as well as experience with the products made and the processes used throughout the world.

- research, some of it carried out at the Nestlé Research Centre near Lausanne (Switzerland), some done in other parts of the world, but all of it co-ordinated by the central research staff.

Nestlé sees its organization in terms of networks, and its networks in terms of its global mandate and the shrinking world. Addressing the Venezuelan Chamber of Industry and Trade, Brabeck clarified his company's position: "When I speak about networks and connections, I do not necessarily mean the complex technology that forms part of it. I mean primarily the reciprocal exchange of minds and ideas. The main emphasis here lies in the significance of human contributions. The corporation provides the environment, so that people can make meaningful contributions to its basic goals. For this reason, they also are given approval for all necessary investments."

Brabeck told his Venezuelan audience that the entire worldwide network of contacts and communication would have to be improved. This had to be done, he said, by augmenting the most important physical communication links, that is to say, the intercontinental telephone lines and satellite connections, with fine-meshed local systems. Mathematical calculations in fact show how this works, and that in this process of rapidly increased linking, the original center loses its importance, or at least its exclusive position. This applies equally to organizations that are structured on the network principle.

Within Nestlé and other global organizations, the flow

of information has shifted direction. It used to be that messages went from the center to the periphery and back again. Now, information can flow in any direction, as connections open up between different markets, different nations, and different workgroups, all of whom can share experiences.

New elements such as local differentiation and world-wide connections are among the changes that have arisen from globalization, and they now determine, to an increasing extent, the goals and structure of corporations.

These general ideas and trends have already led to some practical conclusions at Nestlé, which have redefined the role of the Center and of Nestlé's various markets with respect to the spheres in which both strive to increase value.

Adding value is defined in two ways at Nestlé: first, it means making full use of resources that are already available to the group; second, it can also mean mobilizing new resources through investments, restructuring, and innovation. "Resources" here does not mean just the raw materials or the environment; it refers mainly to the production and marketing technology, the installations and systems. In Production, for example, it could mean the creation of new varieties of cake mixes; in Advertising, linking Buitoni-brand noodles with Maggi-brand sauces; in Sales, placing Nescafé at the point of sale of Nestlé chocolate bars. New resources can also arise from external circumstances, such as the adoption of a common currency in much of Europe, which will allow some production facilities to be merged.

Finally, changes in the range of products offered in a particular market may allow some products to be eliminated or others to be introduced.

Understanding this new definition of added value, according to Brabeck, means seeing how, over time, Nestlé's global presence itself has promoted the creation of a powerful worldwide network of people, knowledge, experience, and relationships with suppliers and customers. As already noted, the company has production facilities in more than seventy countries and sales outlets in just about every country in the world, in addition to research stations in many places. This configuration, in its entirety, creates much greater added value for consumers, personnel, and shareholders than just the sum of the individual contributions of all these installations.

Nestlé has recently made a move to enhance this net effect by creating an intranet that guarantees the horizontal flow of information among the employees of the organization.

At Nestlé, decentralization goes hand in hand with adaptability and sensitivity to local markets. Experience has shown that Nestlé achieves the greatest growth in added value in those markets where its products stand in first place within certain unambiguously defined product categories, such as instant coffee or mineral water. At the same time, Nestlé is aiming for first place—or for a very good second place—in all those market segments in which the corporation is active.

To achieve this, Nestlé aims to conduct its business in a manner at least as satisfactory to its customers as that of its strongest competitor. This means constantly improving its production routines and its products, as a means of ensuring that Nestlé customers will remain loyal and ready to pay an appropriate price for its products.

For Brabeck, consumer orientation does not mean waiting for its customers to tell Nestlé what they want. The corporation has to be proactive in continually tendering new and imaginative products. Brabeck looks for challenges and simultaneous business opportunities in various social trends, such as healthier lifestyles, higher life expectancy and an aging population, spoiled single children, and the rising cost of health care. The real value of a product is ultimately measured by the needs and priorities of consumers. Ideally, the consumers pay lower prices and get more for their money, better quality, and more choice.

That does not necessarily mean homogeneous prices, however. Within the same city a consumer may pay different prices for ice cream, depending on whether he buys it in a supermarket, from a vendor in a public park, or shortly before midnight at a gas station downtown. Despite the strong competition, these retail price differences have actually increased over the years. The consumer is willing to accept them because he recognizes the different levels of service and convenience involved.

Different local eating habits also affect prices. The Dutch, for example, consume nine times as much natural yogurt as the Irish. The result is that the price of natural yogurt is considerably lower in Holland than in Ireland. Similarly, since the consumption of olive oil is very high in Spain, the price there is correspondingly lower than in Germany, where olive oil was practically unknown until just a few years ago. Since it is still considered a specialty item, German consumers are willing to pay a premium.

Quality control is very important to every Nestlé branch. The top priority is the safety of each product in terms of microbiology and toxicity. The other main priority is quality, as perceived by the consumer. To guarantee the highest quality, the entire path of each product, from raw materials to point of sale, is subject to stringent controls.

To gauge consumer perception, Nestlé uses separate blind tests in all its markets. The ultimate goal is for people to perceive the quality of a Nestlé product to be significantly higher than that of the local competition in the proportion of 60:40. Once consumers determine a certain product to be the best, they are asked to provide their reasons. The answers allow the Nestlé staff to improve products in the future. "Our focus as a company, and certainly in the U.S.," says Nestlé USA vice-president communications, Al Stefl, "is to better understand our consumers' needs and then communicate with them through pure communication as well as product development to make sure that they have what they're looking for."

Nestlé's product philosophy does allow for outsourcing, that is, contracting out certain tasks to other companies. Nestlé determines the core activities that have to be under its own control and those that can be safely handed over. A good example is the primary processing of cocoa, which is necessary to make the cocoa usable. It is a part of the production process, but it is unrelated to the ultimate differentiation of cocoa products. This function can, therefore, be carried out by the supplier.

Core competence includes all those tasks that contribute to differentiation and to adding value. In the case of tomato paste, to use a simple example, these factors are not of great importance. Once this product meets certain simple quality standards, it is difficult to differentiate among brands of tomato paste of similar quality.

It is very important to define clearly what core competence consists of in each instance. In this context it is also important to know your markets before you set up your production facilities. They should be able to serve the market amply, but they should also be working efficiently, as close to full capacity as possible.

Nestlé likes to co-operate with related businesses in order to tap *their* core competence. You cannot expect that a supplier of, say, industrial food-drying equipment should know anything about the Nestlé products that will be made with the food dryer, yet by working closely with the supplier, Nestlé can create perfect production units.

Core competence is a subject that often comes up in connection with packaging decisions. The package and the product it contains must always be in harmony. Sometimes, as with pet foods or water, the actual value of the product is relatively minor, but that does not mean that the packaging should be neglected. On the contrary, the box or bottle or bag has to show quality or it will hurt sales. For this reason, Nestlé used to make all its own boxes, but over time the corporation found (or even developed) reliable suppliers, so that this part of the production could be outsourced. Only in developing countries are boxes still made in-house.

The first job of packaging is to maintain and protect all the original qualities of the product. In the case of the yogurt drink LC1 GO, for example, this means that the little bottles must be particularly thick in order to ensure the continued presence of all the beneficial micro-organisms that are guaranteed to be in the drink.

New ways of processing food are constantly being developed as the various manufacturing plants combine the different technologies in use at Nestlé. None of these technological processes has yet reached its full potential. This is well illustrated in the development of powdered foods.

It is an accepted fact that all powdered foods are not equal. Turning food into a powder usually ensures its long-term preservation. It also involves special drying processes that can be very time-consuming. Continuous freeze-drying was first developed in the 1930s, but the process was not applied in industry till the 1960s. To the development of this particular process Nestlé has made a huge contribution. The taste of the various dried foods has come closer and closer to that of the original, liquid form, and the use of energy has been reduced, as the process has gradually improved. The taste of Nescafé is now much closer to that of freshly brewed coffee than when it was first launched.

8

The Art of Branding

"**N**ESCAFÉ IS ALWAYS Nescafé," says Peter Brabeck, "and the real reason is that Nescafé has now been Nescafé for a long time. That is the art of brand management. If we do that right, then the brand never dies, it is always in fashion. It will outlive us all."

These words sum up the current Nestlé philosophy: the product may change, but the brand goes on. Over the past thirty years Brabeck and Maucher have completely overhauled the entire world of Nestlé brand names. "Starting with Nestlé's corporate image, we went through the whole family of brand names," recalls Maucher, "all the way through the hierarchy of brands, the core messages, and the basic designs."

Maucher had always made it clear that at Nestlé, the maintenance of brands would be the exclusive responsibility of top management. Shortly after his arrival at headquarters in Vevey, he reactivated the Nestlé corporate logo of the nest. "You have to endow a multinational concern with warm, emotional elements," says Maucher. "We were lucky that our founder was called Nestlé and that he had developed the wonderful logo with the birds."

Understanding how a brand works is not a totally rational process. Maucher explains that he and Brabeck took time to develop a feeling for each brand, and they gradually built the entire world of Nestlé brands on this kind of emotional understanding. "And the way we did that is for the long term. We intended a brand to retain its characteristics for fifty or a hundred years, always growing in strength and becoming closer to the Nestlé core." Brabeck, he adds, "was my chief visionary."

Some products and brands are very closely associated with Nestlé's image. Among these are chocolate, milk, and nutritional products, and they therefore share the Nestlé name. Other brands have much greater independence. One of these is Maggi. "It is very strong, and the Nestlé nest on the package serves only as an extra value," notes Maucher. "Yet each Nestlé product has those baby birds on the back as a symbol of quality." Nestlé's pet food lines also operate under their own brand name, Nestlé Purina.

"For me, brands are living entities," says Brabeck. "They have life. For me that means that, like any other creature, I have to look after them, I have to feed them, I have to help them grow, I have to give them sufficient substance."

A brand name, to Brabeck, is a bundle of functional and emotional characteristics. If you take only the functional features into account, all you have is a product; you have no ideas, no ideals, and no sense. For this reason it is necessary to find a balance, so that the functional and emotional elements complement each other and form a brand that the consumer finds relevant.

All brands have to be updated from time to time. Freshening a brand is an art, says Brabeck, and for him it consists of making it relevant to new consumer expectations and behaviors. At the same time, the secret is to keep the brand consistent, so that for the consumer the brand remains the same as always; or, to put it more precisely, the relationship between the consumer and the brand remains constant.

One of the contemporary business trends that worries Peter Brabeck is that corporations, by focusing on maximizing short-term gains, do not tend to give their brands enough substance. They suck them dry, ignoring the need for product extensions, improved packaging, or repositioning in the market. Then, suddenly, they are faced with a dying brand that has no further value. You have to invest in a brand to keep it alive.

Lowering the cost of manufacturing Nestlé brand products by an average of 3 percent between 1995 and 2001 allowed the corporation to increase its investment in sales and marketing to almost one-quarter of the average sales price. This was a necessity, according to Brabeck, because in the age of the Internet, brands, and brand advertising, are becoming ever more important.

Many corporations not only fail to invest sufficiently in their brands, but they also fail to distinguish between the requirement for speed in response to customer demand and the search for longevity with respect to the brand image. Maucher knows these mistakes well: "You have to react fast when new technologies are introduced or when consumer tastes change. Ice cream is an example of a product for which you need to introduce many new flavors every year. That simply means that your consumers want a change, and they want a change more frequently with ice cream. It may be sweetness one year; it may be that pink is the fashion color for ice cream. You have to be quick in catching such things."

Nevertheless, whenever you are building a brand, you need ultimately to think long term: "The brand remains exactly the same even when I introduce a new fun product in my ice cream line. Even though we serve completely new consumer tastes with Nescafé, the brand is still the same."

One also has to distinguish among different trends and fads. There are always developments that you just have to let pass by. "That may hurt, but you just wait till the pain is gone," says Maucher. "We cannot, to put it plainly, react to every piece of bullshit that comes along. But when it comes to general movements, technological developments, to changes in consumer tastes or in lifestyle, then we have to move real fast."

For Nestlé the brand itself is a long-term thing. You can occasionally make slight adjustments to modernize the appearance of the brand; you can make small concessions to changing tastes. But you never touch the core of the brand. Maggi has used the same color and the same style of script for a hundred years now, and nothing will be changed.

"Brands mean continuity," says Maucher. "An example of really good brand management is in Coca-Cola. And the company also has done a good job marketing it. They understood that marketing does not consist of broadcasting some silly jingle over radio or television. Coca-Cola knew from the beginning that what matters most in marketing is to make the brand available, to distribute it well. You have to have a presence at the point of consumption, and they do. At every poolside, at every refreshment stand, there is Coke, ready for impulse buying.

"At Nestlé I was often asked why I did not go into the soft drink business. I always answered, 'Either you buy out Coca-Cola or you keep your hands off it.' It's as simple as that."

Peter Brabeck's former role as chief visionary is now played by the American Frank Cella. He has been working for Nestlé for thirty-eight years, and his career is close to the Nestlé career model. His first customers were small stores, which he supplied out of the back of his car. With his growing success and competence, he was entrusted with supplying chain stores.

At the end of the 1960s he led the marketing war for Tasters' Choice's freeze-dried coffee. He then moved to Canada for Nestlé, where he was soon given the task of integrating some newly acquired businesses into the Nestlé realm. He was given the same responsibility in the United States at the end of the 1980s, when it came to making a genuine Nestlé brand out of Carnation. At the end of a second stint in Canada, Cella went to Vevey, the Center, at the end of 1999. There he succeeded Philippe Véron as executive vice president.

To Frank Cella, marketing means offering people the chance to buy Nestlé products wherever they happen to be, at any time. For Cella, good examples of marketing are the People TV spot for Nescafé and the introduction of Tasters' Choice. (The People TV spot showed coffee lovers all around the world in relaxed situations, enjoying Nescafé. The ad could be broadcast internationally because it consisted only of images and music.) People buy Nestlé products every day, Cella argues. Food is not like a car, which you buy only once every five years or so. Therefore, marketing for food has to be a lot more consistent and steady.

Marketing also means selling the consumer a particular feeling, an experience. An example of this is a Nestlé coffee house that was set up in Frankfurt in co-operation with McDonald's. The idea was to serve a variety of different coffee flavors, following the trend set by Starbucks. The product here is far more than just coffee. People don't come for a caffeine fix; they want an experience, a guilt-free break. And for this they are willing to pay more: $3.50 for a mug of coffee.

Taste memories connected to foods and drinks are among the many emotional components that add up to a preference for one brand over another. A well-tied bundle of functional and emotional values guarantees brand power and promotes consumer interest. The goal is always a satisfied consumer. That always leads to customer loyalty, one of the steadiest assets any corporation can have.

Comparing past and current trends, Brabeck sees some important differences. He draws attention to the fact that the transformation of the entire media landscape has profoundly altered the nature of marketing. In the fifties, sixties, and even seventies, he recalls, there was only one television channel per country in most of Europe. The establishment of a second channel was seen as tremendous progress. Those early European channels were in the hands of the governments, and the greatest concern at that time was who had the right to show TV spots, and how many. If you managed to get one of the coveted spots, you could win a large consumer following in one fell swoop. In the United States the presence of only three commercial networks ensured a similar audience concentration.

Today we are looking at a very different picture. There are hundreds of television channels and radio stations, and a myriad of different magazines; the whole scene is highly segmented. The print media are particularly fragmented: it can now take half an hour just to decide which magazine to buy. "To pursue an effective media policy in this environment is not easy," says Brabeck. "It certainly is far more difficult than it used to be."

In the past, the advertising communication models consisted of one sender and millions of recipients. Today's model allows for direct, interactive communication, which is actually far more effective. However, establishing interactive communication with six billion people is not exactly simple. "Today our communications are more efficient because we know how to hit a much smaller target," says

Brabeck. "In the past we used a shotgun approach, but today that is not the case any more. Consequently, marketing is becoming a much more difficult job. Increasingly, it is turning into an art, rather than being a simple set of quantitative tools that you can pick up and learn to use."

This challenge aside, Brabeck doesn't worry about the durability of the Nestlé name: "The Nescafé brand is now 60 years old. The Nestlé brand has been around for 136 years, and I believe that it is still as active and still as relevant as it always was. Those who looked after the brand in the past are gone, but the brand can live on."

GETTING THE NESTLÉ MESSAGE OUT

For its worldwide markets Nestlé has hired five advertising agencies on a permanent basis: McCann Erickson, Lowe Lintas, J. Walter Thompson, Publicis and Ogilvy & Mather. In the United States, Nestlé also works with New York-based Messner Vetere. Nestlé's Japanese market, however, is under the exclusive care of the Dentsu Agency. In many respects Dentsu resembles Nestlé. The advertising agency was founded back in 1901, and by 1999 it employed 5,800 people. Within Japan, Dentsu is represented in all major cities. Its international presence, however, is limited to some partner agencies within the Asian market areas and a Moscow bureau. International businesses continue to find it difficult to hit the right note with their ads in Japan, or to enter into the Japanese media system. For this reason Dentsu holds an unchallenged position within Japan as well as with its Japanese customers throughout the entire Asian area.

Another agency with a long tradition is the French firm Publicis SA, which began operating in Paris in 1926. Publicis was the first agency to advertise over French radio, and also the first to use a questionnaire to undertake market research. Today Publicis employs 10,000 people worldwide and has more than 130 offices in 76 countries. Nestlé has been working with Publicis since 1952, and has thus become one of the agency's oldest customers. As an agency aligned with Nestlé, Publicis works internationally with a $300 million budget, distributed over 40 countries.

Another agency that has a long relationship with Nestlé—going back to 1955—is McCann-Erickson Worldwide. This firm has 15,900 employees in 127 countries. Since 1978, L'Oréal, a member of the Nestlé Group, has also been a customer of McCann-Erickson. As it happens, since 2000 so has the Union Deutscher Lebensmittelwerke, which belongs to Unilever, one of Nestlé's main competitors in Germany.

J. Walter Thompson can surely claim to be the foremost advertising agency in the world, with roots dating back to 1864. In 1868, James Walter Thompson started working as a bookkeeper in a New York advertising agency, which he was able to buy out in 1877 for $500. (He had to pay another $800 for the furniture.) By 1899,

J. Walter was ready to open his first international branch, in London.

This agency also displays a certain degree of Nestlé's entrepreneurial spirit. In 1918 the firm started working for customers in the food industry, namely Libby's and Kraft. In 1986 they opened their first China office. Nestlé Great Britain has been taken care of by J. Walter Thompson since 1930. Their most recent campaign promotes the new orange-flavored KitKat.

9

Land of the Food Giants:
Nestlé's World

LARGE FOOD CORPORATIONS set the global standard for innovative production methods, product safety, market presence, and distribution. In most national markets, however, the multinationals play a lesser role, as compared with the number of food offerings made by their numerous mid-size and small competitors, which distribute their goods regionally or locally.

The large corporations are forced to concentrate on complex food products, on complete frozen menus, or on snacks and other ready-to-eat foods. These products require much greater know-how for their production and offer correspondingly larger margins. The competition and the wealth of ideas around making money from prepared food are enormous. Anuga, the self-styled "Leading Global Exhibition for the Food Industry," shows this with great clarity. In October 2001, 6,205 exhibitors from 95 countries showed their products to 175,000 buyers from 150 countries.

For highly processed foods to sell well, consumer habits

have to change in the way they have already done in North America and Japan. In retail climates such as these, it is the giant food companies that compete against one another, and they have to work harder and harder, as competition intensifies in tighter and tighter markets.

In the year 2000, competition increased dramatically among the big food corporations. They were literally fighting to take over mid-size and small competitors with strong, established markets. That kind of market is important if you want to get the attention of consumers. The aim of the big corporations was to gain second position and move closer to Nestlé, the leader. First Unilever took over its competitor, Bestfoods, and moved from third to second place. Then Philip Morris won the takeover battle for Nabisco to move back into second position.

The American corporation Philip Morris is best known as the world's largest cigarette manufacturer, with brands such as Marlboro, Benson & Hedges, and Chesterfield. In 1999 the tobacco business still made up 60 percent, or $47 billion, of Philip Morris's total sales of $78 billion. After the Nabisco takeover, tobacco still represented about half of its total income, with the food business accounting for about 34 percent. Philip Morris is also active in alcoholic and non-alcoholic beverages.

Philip Morris's food division is combined under Kraft Foods. This concern turned over $27 billion worth of goods in 1999 and was—after Nestlé—the second-largest food producer in the world. The purchase of Nabisco added another $8.3 billion in sales, and so reduced considerably the distance between Philip Morris and Nestlé.

Philip Morris's roots are in the tobacco business, but it diversified into the paper industry in 1957. With the purchase of the Miller Brewing Company at the end of the 1960s, it also started making beer. Today, Miller is the second-largest brewery in the United States. Philip Morris only entered the food industry in 1985. In the ensuing years it bought up companies in various segments of the food business. The two biggest acquisitions were Kraft Foods in 1988 and the purchase in 1990 of the Swiss coffee and chocolate group Jacobs Suchard, for $3.8 billion.

Philip Morris's food division includes, in addition to the Jacobs Suchard brands—Jacobs, Suchard, Milka, and Toblerone—Philadelphia Cream Cheese, Kraft mayonnaise and sauces, Miracle Whip, and Miracoli Pasta. The food division has turned out to be the most valuable part of the agglomerate, with profits diminishing in the cigarette business and the growing number of lawsuits by former smokers, which depress the value of Philip Morris's shares and have a negative effect on profits. The food division generates a profit of more than 15 percent of total sales.

To give all the food products of Philip Morris a unified identity and image, as of June 2000 all sister corporations worldwide were renamed "Kraft." Until then, only the central firm had used that name. No structural changes were involved. In the food industry it is rumored that the name change was made in reaction to the successful brand strategies of Nestlé. Bernhard Huber, Kraft Chief for Germany and Austria, stated that this was just the first shot in a developing battle for the leading position in the food business.

Apparently even at Kraft the leadership has finally realized that a uniform image for the firm and special care for the brand names lends them much greater credibility. Huber also stated in May 2000 that Kraft had to become "global," in the sense of adjusting its organization to take local cultures into account. This practice has been routine at Nestlé for decades.

Philip Morris won the takeover fight for Nabisco that went on for months. Up for sale were both Nabisco Group Holdings, the mother group, and Nabisco Holdings, which encompassed the food division and of which a full 80 percent was owned by Nabisco Group Holdings. Nabisco had already shed R.J. Reynolds, the tobacco company, known for the brands Camel and Winston. The first bidder for Nabisco was the investor Carl Icahn, who already held 9.5 percent of the mother group. Another twelve bidders then entered the scene. Most of these wanted to buy only the food division.

Philip Morris did not want to buy the Nabisco Group holding company any more than the others did, but it had to purchase it in order to obtain the food division. Thus it ended up buying into the potential lawsuits against the Nabisco Group's former tobacco division, R.J. Reynolds. No doubt Philip Morris was feeling itself under heavy pressure after Unilever purchased its competitor, Bestfoods, and thus moved into second place, after Nestlé. Philip Morris paid a total of $14.9 billion for Nabisco.

Nabisco Holdings, the food division, is the U.S. market leader for crackers and cookies. It owns the brands Oreo, Ritz, and Chips Ahoy! Its product range also includes Planters Peanuts, Life Savers, and A1 Steak Sauce. At this time, more than 70 percent of Nabisco's sales are made in the United States, and as board president James Kilts put it, the business should expand into Asia. As for Europe—where up to now Nabisco has had only one branch, in Spain—a joint venture is being built with United Biscuits. This company leads the European market in cookies and baked goods.

A concern like Philip Morris, which owns tobacco and alcohol divisions, will never be able to represent the concept of wellness with the same credibility as Nestlé, which rid itself of its wineries twenty years ago. In Europe, Kraft is playing up its American image and also maintains the American flavor of its foods, because these things correspond to the youthful lifestyle people are leaning towards. Nestlé too serves this trend, but it does it with a message of quality that has a strong national flavor. The fight between these giants is not happening in remote boardrooms but in the supermarket, and consumers are the referees.

Unilever is another of Nestlé's international competitors. A corporation with Dutch and British roots, it originally made margarine and soap, and arose in 1929 out of the union of Margarine Unie and Lever Brothers. Today it is among the leading international producers of consumer goods, with two core areas: food on the one hand, and laundry and cleaning products, personal care, and cosmetics on the other. Unilever owns brands like Dove soap, Pepsodent toothpaste and Calvin Klein perfumes.

To concentrate on these core areas Unilever has divested itself of its packaging and special chemicals businesses. It is still seen primarily as a washing product manufacturer, but by now somewhat more than half of its sales derive from food products, among them Ragu sauces, Lipton beverages, and Iglu frozen foods.

For a long time, people in the food business considered Unilever to be too fat, too lazy, and too slow. It maintained too many brands without enough global presence. In 1999, Unilever lost 4.3 percent of its sales.

The new co-chairman of the corporation, Anthony Burgmans and Niel Fitzgerald, decided to take drastic action. At the beginning of 2000 they declared that Unilever would reduce its range of products from 1,600 to 400, since 1,000 of the corporation's brands contributed only 8 percent to its total sales. They are planning to close 100 of the corporation's 350 factories worldwide, and to let go about 25,000 workers. Such measures would strike Nestlé's Peter Brabeck as a personal defeat. He would much rather work hard on improving business on a daily basis. That way, he says, you can live up to your public responsibilities as a business.

Burgmans and Fitzgerald further announced that, in future, Unilever would focus its business activity on the profitable brands, like Magnum ice cream, Lipton tea, Calvin Klein perfumes, and Dove soap. In addition, the new co-chairmen created a new division called Vitality, devoted entirely to healthful nutrition. Some people say that this move is modeled on National Strategic Division, which has been in operation since 1997.

The restructuring of Unilever is expected to take three to five years, and to strengthen its earnings. Burgmans and Fitzgerald have also stated that acquisitions will play a large part in his future plans.

Unilever has already made at least two acquisitions, both of interest mostly to the North American market: Unilever bought Ben & Jerry's ice cream in 2000 for $326 million, and the diet product maker Slimfast for $2.3 billion. Slimfast grossed $611 million in 1999 and shows a growth rate of 20 percent; only 6 percent of its sales are generated outside the United States, however. With the purchase of Ben & Jerry's, Unilever is reinforcing its position as the world leader in upscale ice cream products. Until recently, Ben & Jerry's was available only in the United States, where it achieved $237 million in sales. Now Unilever wants to give the brand a worldwide presence.

In June 2000 it was announced that Unilever was taking over the United States sauce manufacturer Bestfoods for $20.3 billion. Bestfoods owns the brands Knorr, Pfanni, Mazola, Mondamin, Grossman and Ubena, Skippy peanut butter, and Hellman's mayonnaise, as well as Dextro Energen. Knorr and Pfanni are in stiff competition with Maggi, and Hellman's is a rival to Nestlé's Thomy brand.

The merger of Unilever and Bestfoods creates a giant

concern with a total turnover of $52.3 billion and net profits of $6.2 billion. The food divisions of these corporations generate combined sales of $29.1 billion; $20.47 billion of this comes from Unilever, $8.6 billion from Bestfoods. This new power in the food business has shoved Kraft out of second place, which it held for a long time.

Unilever's acquisition strengthens mainly its North American sales. In the United States in 1999, the corporation had sales of $2.3 billion, including income from its household and personal care divisions. In the same year Nestlé grossed $10 billion in the U.S. Bestfoods now adds $1.9 billion in annual sales to Unilever's American business. In Europe, Bestfoods' sales reached $3.6 billion dollars, in Asia $370 million, and in Latin America $1.1 billion.

Unilever's position has been enhanced worldwide in the area of culinary products with the addition of spreads, teas, and ice creams. The new product lines are all highly processed—and profitable. Moreover, they are in line with the current trend towards convenience. Unilever plans to eliminate some sauces and soup brands, but in its move to take over a share of the market Bestfoods will play a major role.

People in the industry agree that one very important point about the acquisition of Bestfoods is that it will allow Unilever to strengthen its position in emerging markets, which is where the greatest growth potential now lies. Up to now, Unilever could manage to make only 20 percent of its sales in these markets. The reason is that so many of its own products—margarine and frozen foods, for example—

require refrigeration. The soups and oils of Bestfoods have a much better future in developing countries.

Some analysts consider the price Unilever paid for Bestfoods excessive, at $20.3 billion. Unilever also had to take over Bestfoods' debt of $4 billion, making the deal even more expensive. In fact, Unilever will save $750 million a year through its merger with Bestfoods. Employees and unions fear that the restructuring will involve even more cutbacks than originally announced. Around the world, Unilever employs a total of 255,000 people.

After the battles over Nabisco and Bestfoods, experts in the food industry predicted a new wave of mergers. Candidates for takeover include Campbell Soup, H.J. Heinz, and General Mills, the breakfast cereal maker, which has been working with Nestlé since 1989 and also owns Gatorade and Quaker Oats. Potential buyers were identified, among them, inevitably, Nestlé.

Then, in mid-July 2000, there was an announcement by Paul Walsh, CEO of Diageo, a U.S. conglomerate, that the company would now concentrate on making spirits and beer, and was ready to sell Burger King and Pillsbury. The latter firm, which makes ready-to-use-dough and also owns Häagen-Dazs ice cream, has been sold to General Mills, in a deal that left Diageo a 32.6 percent share of the newly formed, merged corporation. Over time, however, this share will be reduced to zero. This merger has moved General Mills/Pillsbury into seventh place among the world's largest food producers.

It is interesting to note that Nestlé worked in co-operation with both of these corporations—in breakfast cereals with General Mills, and with Pillsbury in terms of ice cream. It was in 1999 that Nestlé formed Ice Cream Partners USA, with Pillsbury, a joint venture that distributes both Häagen-Dazs and Nestlé ice creams in the United States. In the meantime Nestlé has acquired the other 50 percent of the shares in Ice Cream Partners, as well as the licence to use the Häagen-Dazs brand in the USA and Canada.

One thing is clear when we look at Nestlé and all its competitors: despite their size, none of these giants can act freely, that is, without encountering controls or being watched. The battle for market segments is expressed in fractions of a percentage point; the price wars are fought in terms of pennies. Consumer behavior is not static, and product ideas are taken up by the competition within months or even weeks.

The food business plays out its scenarios by its own rules, and the points are counted in the public arena of the supermarkets. But the actors who cause these events are within each of the corporations. It is the written and unwritten rules—those that govern these concerns and bind together their leadership and their employees—that, in the last analysis, determine their achievements.

10

Globalization: Do the Multinationals Have the World by the Throat?

JACK WELCH OF GENERAL Electric was no doubt correct when he stated that whatever counts in the corner grocery store is the same thing that counts in a power plant or a medical system. This is true enough, but it is not the whole story. Public expectations and the criteria used for judgment are much less forgiving in the case of a mammoth corporation.

The managers of multinational concerns have to remain sensitive to all social changes that take place, even beyond the borders of their own empire. Should they fail to keep up and to respond with alacrity and tact, they will sooner or later face problems such as Nestlé still has to deal with in the areas of baby food and genetically modified ingredients. With respect to the former, Nestlé was criticized for marketing baby formula in developing nations. With the latter, it was condemned for interfering with nature. (The issues will be discussed in detail in Chapter 12.)

Nestlé's example clearly shows that the public punishes perceived bad judgment on the part of multinationals more severely and for a much longer time than would be the case for a small company, or even a government, political party, union, or non-governmental organization (NGO). Transnational corporations are made to pay dearly for what are sometimes relatively small failures in marketing and communications.

As a result of these controversies, Nestlé became a symbol of all that was seen to be negative about globalization in general. This was particularly so in Germany, Switzerland, Great Britain, and to some extent North America, and it continues to be so for the NGOs. In this type of situation, neither the realities of the corporation's activities nor the actual facts on any particular point have very much to do with anything that is said against the corporation. What really influences the public's view of Nestlé is the ability of anti-globalization forces to unite various divergent interest groups behind their cause, and to stimulate them to bolster one another with an ongoing barrage of new—and also quite outdated—information, opinions, and claims.

In this ongoing effort the Internet plays a major role, functioning like some sort of super brain. What has once been placed on a Web site is never lost, corrected, or updated. Differentiation between yesterday and today is virtually suspended. The Internet has another important feature that is relevant here: it allows anyone to render any subject as emotional and topical as possible, and to disseminate information about it to any number of recipients around the globe. All this can be done with only a small amount of trouble and expense, and the quality of the information thus sent out is subject to no controls whatsoever.

One of the problems faced by a corporation that has become the target of the anti-globalization NGOs arises from the diversity of the opponents that are loosely allied against it. Precisely because the different anti-globalization groups have little in common, they take a very limited interest in one another's causes; none seems to examine very carefully what the others have actually said, and why. They use one another's arguments, but they never seem to check them. Any statement that serves the cause is accepted as important and correct.

It is this unquestioned acceptance that a corporation under attack has to address. Misinformation has to be corrected, misunderstandings have to be clarified, and the facts in the corporation's favor have to be adduced. Only with clear, honest communications does a corporation under attack have any chance of finding acceptance for its position.

NGOs do not have a unified structure or a common goal. In 1990 there were 6,000 such organizations; now there are 29,000 acting globally. Their size varies from one-man outfits to groups with thousands of members. Since in this game size is irrelevant, even tiny interest groups can become international opinion leaders. Nor does it matter how much support such an organization can actually muster among the wider population for it to influence public opinion.

The positions of Nestlé's various critics might be summarized as follows:

1. **Opponents of capitalism and of the market economy:** Nestlé is a global enterprise. Globalization means uncontrolled economic power that thrives by exploiting helpless national governments. The negative impacts of globalization are disastrous for the population of much of the world. The products of such economic giants have to be boycotted.

2. **Environmental groups:** Nestlé manufactures foods by industrial processes. Such products are bad for consumers. The preferred alternative to industrial food production is organically grown food, the fruits of environmentally friendly agriculture. Gene technology is the central, emotionally loaded subject in this critique of Nestlé.

3. **Those who still oppose Nestlé on the baby-food issue:** Nestlé violates generally accepted human rights and ethical and socio-political principles. The central theme here is the health of infants and small children, a continuation of the campaigns of the seventies and eighties.

The anti-corporate movement has quickly developed into a protective umbrella for a diverse collection of interests and goals. It offers its followers the opportunity to criticize every conceivable aspect of Western society, and directs their animus against easy targets, including name brands of every sort.

In her best-selling book *No Logo*, Canadian journalist Naomi Klein takes issue with the tremendous amounts of money that large corporations spend on promoting their brands. What would happen if the multinationals stopped spending on advertising is not discussed. Klein also objects to multinational corporations that manufacture their products cheaply in Asia, use child labor to cut their expenses, and exploit the natural world in distant lands. That she should thus pillory corporations that act in this manner is good and praiseworthy, but what she fails to make clear is that corporations act in very different ways. Because of this important omission, she leaves her readers with the impression that *all* makers of name-brand products do so in Asia by means of child labor.

Other critics train their guns closer to home. "Globalization does not benefit the broad masses," says Mark Weisbrot, one of the directors of the Center for Economic Policy in Washington. According to Weisbrot, many people are excluded from the benefits of global commerce not only in the developing countries but also in the highly developed, industrialized countries. Weisbrot justifies his thesis by saying that in the United States, median real income has not shown any growth in the last twenty-six years. This must mean that the average employee did not participate in the economic growth that prevailed during that period.

Weisbrot finds the same stagnation, and even regression, in average income within the developing world. In his opinion, nothing but the complete collapse of global planning would allow for international development that could in any way be called socially just.

Certain journalists in some economic periodicals go even further. They blame corporate misbehavior for *all* the ills the world is facing, namely, unemployment, poverty, economic catastrophes, devaluation of currencies, and the persistent chasm between the poor and the rich countries.

Some predict the formation of a new "Globalization International," quite unrelated to the *Communist Manifesto* but rather an unusual alliance of activists from the Right and the Left. The journalists suggest that this union could include politicians, environmentalists, Third World groups, farmers' representatives, churches, unions, and consumer organizations. This new Globalization International would function as a means of expression for all the diffused anxieties felt by the world's population.

A completely different and more hopeful view is expounded by Harvard economist Robert J. Barro. He shows in his study *Determinants of Democracy* that the chief barrier to democratization is poverty. An expanding economy, he claims, benefits primarily people in the lower- and middle-income ranges. These population segments are granted improved opportunities to better their lives and to organize their interests. Direct investment in the emerging markets, for Barro, goes hand in hand with employment, education, and civil rights for the masses.

Professor Jeffrey A. Frankel of Harvard University lends support to this view in his working paper *Globalization of the Economy*, published by the National Bureau of Economic Research in Cambridge, Massachusetts. Frankel asserts that the effects of globalization on various economies are far less significant than either the supporters or the opponents of globalization have claimed. According to him, other factors, such as a common language and the prevailing laws, have far more impact than global economic arrangements.

Nestlé was made an early symbol of globalization. Multinationals, the enthusiastic agents of globalization, have come to be seen as the villains of our age by those who—quite rightly—object to the many injustices and problems that have arisen from this historic development. However, globalization is a general trend, the final impact of which has not yet been determined. Creating scapegoats is hardly an effective means of bringing about change. Genuine research and open discussion would constitute a much more important—though more difficult—intellectual effort.

Here, in a few words, are the current arguments against globalization: Multinationals are perfect but soulless machines designed to maximize, in the shortest possible time, the return on the capital investment of the shareholders of the conglomerate. How this is achieved and who is really paying for it are matters of no concern. There is no room for human beings in the endless columns of numbers that constitute financial statistics. Employees are interchangeable, rationalized components. Customers count only in terms of numbers, as potential sales. They are manipulated by subliminal messages to make a never-ending series of purchases of basically inessential goods of dubious quality. In other respects they are helpless against transnational capitalism.

The clear winners, when this doom-and-gloom scenario is accepted, are the aforementioned NGOs. Thilo Bode, the former head of Greenpeace International, has been quoted as saying, "The NGOs are more influential than ever before." Recent history bears him out. In 1998, six hundred NGOs united to stop the MAI agreement proposed by the OECD member states—essentially, the developed world—which was to set new ground rules for all foreign investments made by those countries.

Yet another demonstration of the NGOs' power came when representatives from these groups were invited to participate in the discussions of the 30th World Economic Forum 2000, in Davos, Switzerland. This new level of recognition, however, was insufficient for many NGOs. Two organizations that favor international development launched an international publicity campaign dubbed "The Public Eye on Davos." They demanded new rules for conducting the World Economic Forum. Altogether, 150 NGOs from thirty-nine countries stood behind the list of accusations, among them:

- The World Economic Forum maintains an undemocratic, elitist approach to decision making that is no longer acceptable to today's informed and concerned public.
- This approach promotes economic policies that deepen the chasm between rich and poor, curtail the

space for democratic action, and destroy the environment.
- Inasmuch as the World Economic Forum is dealing with the media within set subject categories, it is actually managing information; this prevents full critical reporting of the event.

It is impossible to respond objectively to the second point, for it is a generalized accusation against the World Economic Forum and its guests, among them Nestlé. As to the first point, the summit is definitely elitist. The NGOs that were invited will be aware of this, since it has undoubtedly increased their own prestige. Unfortunately, it is also true that not all journalists have access to the Forum. Furthermore, journalists too can belong to elites. Those who were present at the Economic Forums in the last few years have certainly displayed no solidarity with their excluded colleagues, but have made full use of the advantages the inside track gave them.

Other opponents of globalization are less complex in their attacks, but equally muddled in their thinking. Mcspotlight.org is a British initiative, part of an autonomous network that fights against McDonald's and other multinationals, including Nestlé.

Under the heading "What is Wrong with Nestlé?" we find "the support of brutal and repressive regimes." The reason given for this assertion is that the Nestlé Group maintains branches in Brazil, China, Colombia, Egypt,

El Salvador, Guatemala, India, Indonesia, Kenya, Lebanon, Mexico, Papua New Guinea, the Philippines, Senegal, Sri Lanka, Turkey, and South Africa. In fact, this complaint is directed not just against Nestlé but also against all these countries.

Suppose that all of these countries were in fact run by "regimes," that is, government without distribution of power, without parliaments or judicial systems. Would it not be the first duty of the elected governments of the democratic countries to break off diplomatic relations and stop all aid to these "regimes"? Yet the leaders of the free world, when they meet with members of the governing bodies of these "regimes," do not even avoid group pictures. Nor is Nestlé by any means the only multinational to do business in these nations.

Mcspotlight.com has more complaints to lodge about Nestlé. Among other things, it claims that in 1989, Nestlé laid off forty workers in its factory in Caçapava, Brazil. Also, in 1993, Nestlé refused to process fifteen tons of radioactively contaminated milk powder that had been sent from Poland to Sri Lanka. The shipment was instead returned to its country of origin, where it was supposed to be destroyed. In this, Nestlé's actions were in accordance with accepted international practice, so why Mcspotlight.com thinks it is a problem is not clear.

The "Declaration de Berne" works by standards that are considerably more clear and concrete. In a thorough study of the dealings of Swiss businesses with the Suharto clan, Nestlé is mentioned, along with most other large Swiss firms, and indeed the government of Switzerland. Nestlé has a subsidiary, which it jointly owns with the Bimantara Group, which in turn is owned by a son and a son-in-law of Suharto. It is very useful and praiseworthy to lay bare such connections, even though it does not affect the basic economic realities of this world, namely, that in every country economic decisions are ultimately tied to certain personalities.

These examples show that it is difficult to find or identify actual information or justified complaints or claims amongst the multitude of statements published—mostly over the Internet—by the huge network of concerned organizations. In the United States, for example, there is a strong anti-China alliance between consumer groups and labor unions. The unions worry about the loss of domestic jobs to cheap Chinese labor. Naturally, corporations that produce in China are attacked, including Nestlé.

Since there is no world government, Nestlé's actions take place within the context of the nation states in which its operating companies are, that is to say, in relation with local consumers, employees, and government institutions. Peter Brabeck sees all businesses as a part of the social structure of any given country. Therefore, he believes that businesses have to live up to certain responsibilities, and cannot ignore or oppose the social environment in which they operate. All this does not mean, however, that Nestlé has to sacrifice its own principles.

The much-criticized model of the free market economy appeals to Brabeck precisely because it works without requiring selfless actions on the part of any of the participants. Thus Nestlé's long-term investment in the coffee plantations in the Yunnan area of China was not motivated by a desire to help the poor farmers of that region. Nestlé did it simply because it needed the raw materials produced there. Nonetheless, Nestlé's actions had the effect of improving the lives of thousands of families and of reducing the population's flight to the cities, which is one of the major problems that China is currently facing.

When Nestlé is criticized for co-operating with governments that are notorious for giving low priority to human rights issues, Brabeck responds by saying that if Nestlé dealt only with countries that are not targeted by organizations such as Amnesty International, then the corporation could not even do business in Switzerland, its country of origin.

"Nestlé is willing to do business in any country that offers it the opportunity to do so," Brabeck says, "but it does business at its own risk, according to its own management principles, by its own standards of quality and safety, and through its own methods of dealing with employees and partners. This is the contribution Nestlé can make. Using these principles, Nestlé can contribute to the prosperity of the countries that offer it a chance to do business. By this competition, it forces local suppliers and commercial and financial partners, as well as local governments, to improve their own procedures."

Nestlé does not consider it necessary to judge or to affect decisions made by the governments of the countries in which it does business, unless such decisions have a direct and concrete impact on the corporation's chances of success in the country in question. Where Nestlé's economic existence becomes impossible, the corporation will simply withdraw from that particular economic arena. This has happened in only a few cases, because Nestlé and its employees are unusually persistent, patient, and tough. In this they resemble the farmers of the mountainous terrain of Switzerland, Nestlé's home base. Experience has shown that persistent staying power usually pays off.

Yet the imagination of some governments has no limits, and it has happened that one African government set impossible rules. It tried to set minimum production levels for Nestlé, while also limiting its access to certain raw materials and, at the same time, trying to set the sales price for Nestlé products. To cap it all, government-owned businesses, supported by tax money, were set up in order to offer competition to Nestlé. None of this made any economic sense, so the corporation withdrew.

Helmut Maucher regards globalization as the central subject of our day. "Many countries have stopped opposing direct investments by multinational concerns and are now actively vying for this kind of capital investment. Such private foreign investment is desired for good reasons. They have all had a chance to see that this is the easiest way to develop their countries."

Continuing in a slightly different vein, Maucher says: "What is negative is what I call 'yes-but' capitalism. What this means is that everyone is for a free market economy and for private property, but at the same time, people want to make it hard for capitalists. They want to make rules and regulations to limit businesses, they exaggerate the product liabilities, they want to forbid certain kinds of advertising, or they oppose all rationalization of production. Yes-but capitalism is a creeping phenomenon and it can be dangerous to economic order."

Maucher does not hide his anger about this matter. "They tell us, you are not allowed to do business with China any more because they violate human rights. If you continue, we will apply pressures. Now there are certain principles we have always adhered to at Nestlé: we do not want any child labor and we refuse to deal with suppliers that use child labor, no matter how cheap their goods. But to leave China would be absurd."

For Maucher, the solution is clear. "When people do not have to fight hunger on a daily basis any more, they develop new values. Then, greater prosperity arises and, with it, more cultural activities, more education, and a greater sensibility to these matters. Out of that, democracy can arise. With growing democratization, there is a growing respect for the rights of the individual, which we all want to maintain, after all. But all this happens in concrete steps. It does not happen because people make declarations. If we at Nestlé, together with a few other concerns, are able to make sure that hunger in China is reduced each year by a certain measure, if we manage to help raise the standard of living a little, then there is no political party that can prevent people becoming more concerned about these human rights issues."

Maucher recognizes the communications problems

that arise from this approach to the increasing complexity of society. "It takes time to show how globalization makes indirect contributions to prosperity, how it opens to the underdeveloped countries better access to world markets, or how, in the last few years, globalization helped to free 500 to 600 million people from abject poverty. All this is a lot harder to explain than the simple slogans of the critical groups. At this time, I am beginning to see a danger, namely, that good developments will be made much more difficult or even prevented."

Despite these seemingly harsh words, Maucher has a subtle view of the process of globalization, and his position may actually be quite close to those critics of globalization who are not simply rejecting it, but are looking for practical solutions. "Of course, you cannot let globalization simply happen. Regulation is needed ... By that I mean regulations that must provide the framework within which the market economy, the free economy, can function."

Within each country the state lays the groundwork for a free economy and maintains its smooth functioning, all the while protecting and guaranteeing individual rights. The state does this by creating and enforcing a set of consistent rules and actions. In other words, the free market cannot be left to function by itself, as it has a tendency to form oligopolies and even monopolies, which shifts the balance of power. The free market, that is, competition, has an inherent tendency to destroy itself by eliminating all rivals. Thus the state must reach into the market and make regulatory moves. And the market has to be curtailed in its powers as well, to prevent it from changing, or significantly altering, the mechanism of supply and demand.

Large corporations are often accused of pursuing policies of pure self-interest. This is the main reason for opposing them, and it is the criterion that legitimizes the campaigns against them. Maucher's thinking, however, would surprise his opponents, who would have a hard time fitting his ideas into their generalizations. "Globalization happens in terms of transitions. Transitions are always painful because they cause problems. Therefore, we have to monitor and support these transitions; we cannot let them happen and just say catch as catch can. We need rules to shore up the transitions; we need certain social measures to support those affected. Only if we can do this will globalization turn out to be a win-win setup for all concerned, for the developing countries as well as for the industrialized ones.

"What we still have to manage now are the dislocations that occur in the process of transition. That is where the problems arise. And to mitigate these problems we need more co-operation among all parts of the globe, whether we like it or not. We need the United Nations, but with more powers and more agencies that can monitor and regulate things on a world scale.

"On the whole I believe that a world economy and businesses that act on a global scale make all of us stronger in the end...The more closely the economies of nations are interlinked, the more difficult it will be to suddenly turn around and start shooting at others. Today, the technology of communications makes everything so transparent that no nation can close itself off, not even the Chinese...I think that things are moving forward, towards more peace, more prosperity, and more protection for human rights. But the road there is paved with problems because such processes never run their course smoothly."

In the context of globalization, corporate size is a constant and fundamental theme. Within Nestlé itself the subject is discussed again and again, and the advantages of magnitude are weighed against its drawbacks. Are the corporation's dimensions still manageable, still reasonable? Is it getting too large? In Maucher's view, the matter of competition is more important than the question of a concern's magnitude. Much of the discussion around size is sheer mysticism, according to him. In any case, laws, competition, control agencies, and publicity will always curtail size.

Maucher himself would plead for a practical solution, namely, for allowing each branch of the economy, each form of production, to work out its own optimum size. To have international competition, a certain size is indispensable. The same is true if a company is to have the necessary capital base to invest in research and technological development. In other areas, for specialized products, for purely local businesses, and for service industries, there remain many possibilities in terms of size. Variety is important.

People who are hungry and ill or disabled by deprivation have to be fed before they can take an interest in their external conditions. Hungry people are primarily interested in eating. As long as this basic need is not met, everything else will remain unimportant. Citizens of fully industrialized countries have little conception of how cumbersome and time-consuming it can be in other parts of the world just to find the daily food needed to maintain life.

In West Africa, for example, women who live in small towns and villages can spend the entire day just buying a few basic staples. In some places, fresh vegetables and meat are never available in sufficient amounts, and quality and selection is bad. If the nearest market is, say, three hundred kilometers away, the women of the village will get on a bus in the early morning for a five- to six-hour trip to the nearest market. It will be well after dark when they return home.

People who live under such conditions take little interest in issues like gene technology or the environment. A better food supply or delivery system, however, would save them time. This freed-up time could then be used for productive work, which might in the long run form the basis for a slight increase in their standard of living—their "prosperity," if you will.

To such people, "prosperity" does not mean looking for a house in the suburbs, a second car, or a second vacation each year. In most parts of the world it only means covering the cost and maintaining the flow of the basic necessities of life. A worker with the International Chamber of Commerce told the author that in a Chinese village he can immediately tell which farmers are supplying Nestlé with milk: their houses all have roofs that keep the rain out. A regular income made the necessary repairs possible.

Likewise, the Filipino coffee growers who sell their crops to Nestlé can probably afford a moped. This makes them mobile and lessens their dependence on the dealers who visit their village. Prosperity begins in small ways, just as it did in nineteenth-century Europe and North America.

It is difficult for those who live in developed countries to imagine what life in the emerging economies is like. For one thing, everyone in those countries is used to the sight of the Western or international lifestyle juxtaposed on extreme and public poverty. This contrast and all economic shades in between are manifest in everyday life; poverty is not seen as a public shortcoming. In Europe, on the other hand, the poor are kept hidden away as much as possible. And in America, everyone still believes that it is possible for a dishwasher to become a millionaire.

In the so-called emerging countries there is a shared consciousness that it is impossible to help everyone at once. People also tend to understand that each individual step taken affects everyone around. Prosperity does not mean that money is hoarded. Whoever is able to earn money will improve his or her own life by spending it, and by so doing will provide a chance for others to earn some money as well.

During the next twenty years a major factor in global development will be the emergence into the third millennium of the developing countries of Asia and Latin America. The significance of these areas has already grown as compared with the emerging economies of other areas, such as Africa. During the last twenty years, 500 million people have taken the first step out of poverty, and into the consumer society and access to manufactured goods.

Back in 1989, 80 percent of Nestlé's business was transacted with just 16 percent of the world's population, that is, with the people who lived in the industrialized countries outside the realm of communism. At that time only 18 percent of all Nestlé's sales were to the 52 percent of humanity that live in emerging countries. Today, Nestlé does 30 percent of all its business within the emerging nations, and with respect to food sales, it achieves the highest rates of growth there. And this is by no means the end of this expansion: it is in the emerging nations that the greatest population growth is taking place.

These developments bring us to the heart of a major dilemma. Will the people of these developing countries be used to swell the profits of the multinationals and the wealth of their shareholders, thus widening the gap between rich and poor? Or will they have a real chance to participate in the prosperity they are helping to create?

Different multinationals will have different answers to this fundamental question, and their answers will in no small part depend on what they are producing. The legitimacy of the methods and aims of many multinationals is dubious. This is certainly true of the oil producers who pump the black gold of Africa out of its soil. It is equally true of the food corporations that use industrial processes to sweep the fish out of the coastal waters of the African continent in order to make cheaper frozen fish products for the European and American markets. They also make fish meal to feed to pigs, cattle, and chickens, in order to keep the price of meat low in the developed countries. It is important to point out that this is not the way Nestlé does business.

So-called brand-net enterprises, of which Nike, the athletic shoe producer, is a good example, also differ fundamentally from Nestlé. Their business structure is totally unlike Nestlé's, and therefore the total impact of their enterprise on its environment is different as well. Nike is headquartered in the United States, and it is there that every important marketing decision is made. Production, by contrast, can take place anywhere, as long as low wages keep costs down and the quality of the products is acceptable. When costs rise above a certain level, the company folds its tents and moves to another country. The beautiful products—high-end designer footwear for sport and fashion—are sold wherever the best profits are to be made. Some shoes are retailed in emerging countries, but the corporation could never sustain its factories in those locations on the money it makes selling its shoes there.

As we have seen, Nestlé operates in a completely different way. It makes food for the countries in which it manufactures. Whenever possible, it uses indigenous raw materials and employs local workers. In any one country Nestlé's individual manufacturing units are never larger than those of the local competition, including the non-global, medium-sized players. Nestlé tries in each place to meet the needs of the people living there. This is achieved by introducing "popularly positioned products," whose price is kept competitive. Using local raw materials and packaging also keeps prices down.

Peter Brabeck likes to talk about the unique mission of the food industry, namely, to provide all human beings with healthy food, while at the same time giving shareholders a reasonable return on investment. This twofold intention has been the philosophy at Nestlé as it has grown into an international leader within the food industry, and it will continue to be the principle by which Nestlé operates.

Brabeck leaves no doubt that Nestlé has multiple responsibilities, both social and ethical, and that it is fully aware of this fact. In his view, it is of paramount importance for an economic enterprise to create prosperity, because this benefits humanity as a whole. In terms of corporate management, this means making a profit. He points out that making a profit is the goal of any business. Furthermore, he adds, a business is the only social unit that is in a position to create prosperity.

Corporate profits is a touchy subject. Nestlé may succeed in convincing you that it does not flood emerging markets with products made in Europe, or destroy the labor markets of industrialized countries by importing foods made in Asia or Africa. You can rest assured that Nestlé's plants in developing countries will not cause any factories in the industrialized countries to shut down. However, none of this changes the fact that Nestlé makes impressive corporate profits—a circumstance that does not sit well with Nestlé's critics.

One objection to corporate profits that is frequently

raised is that it is only a very small group—the shareholders—who share in the wealth that is created. But we have to ask the person who raises this objection, Is a global market economy something you want? And if not, what alternative would you offer? Neither socialism, as it has actually played itself out in the real world, nor the return to alternative land-communes has shown any tangible results. No critic of the global market economy has come up with an alternative that can be implemented on a global scale. And any alternative system would still have to yield profits, in order to fuel the efforts needed to get the job done.

Brabeck offers the following calculations, based on 1997 figures: In a good year Nestlé clears a net profit of 5 to 6 percent of total sales, which in 1997 amounted to 70 billion Swiss francs, or $42.7 billion. Before any profit can be calculated and paid out, however, Nestlé has to pay 1.85 billion francs in Swiss corporate taxes. Then, of its 4 billion francs in profits, Nestlé has to pay 1.4 billion in dividends, of which the Swiss government will automatically keep 35 percent in further taxes.

At this point critics will object that all this tax money benefits only Switzerland, a country that can hardly be called poor, and that the rest of the world receives nothing. Yet in the same year Nestlé spent about $11.2 billion on all the raw materials the corporation used to make its products—milk, cocoa, coffee, and so on. Hundreds of thousands of small farmers and their families around the world were able to sell their crops to the corporation. Another $3.7 billion was spent on packing materials.

For the 230,000 employees of the corporation, Nestlé paid out $7.1 billion in wages, salaries, and benefits. All along the line between its production and the retailing of its final products, Nestlé maintains a chain of "prosperity wells." And the flow of prosperity does not end there. In all, Nestlé adds considerably to the security of the lives of millions of people through its worldwide production of food.

Thus, the 1.4 billion Swiss francs that were paid out in dividends to about 200,000 shareholders in 1997 represent only the tip of the prosperity iceberg. Critics of capitalism also tend to forget that dividends do not represent speculative gains, in the nature of lottery winnings. They are the return on participation in the risk of doing business—a risk that in Nestlé's case is, admittedly, not very high.

"This is what the process of generating prosperity is all about," says Brabeck. "A company like Nestlé, which was forced to report a loss only twice in its 135-year history, creates prosperity through productivity; it does so in the billions." Brabeck answers those who are tempted to disparage the fundamental importance of material prosperity by reminding them that money provides security in old age, pays for education, makes possible artistic achievement, and offers help to the needy.

Nestlé approaches the creation of value in the following ways:

- Nestlé offers products that the consumer can value as both functional and appealing.
- Nestlé will never forget that its business partners

have to be able to share in the value the corporation creates.

- On a broader scale, Nestlé creates value for the economy and the society in which the corporation happens to be active.

All of these activities only make sense, however, if in the long and short run, shareholders are rewarded for their participation.

There are many misunderstandings concerning the globalization of markets. Many organizations—including some large corporations—see globalization as merely multiplying what already existed, that is to say, international trade and investment. A few well-run corporations see globalization as a fundamental change; and they believe that, without a clear concept of the world market, it is impossible to achieve success in this new arena.

For Brabeck, globalization means new opportunities and new challenges. Nestlé does not share the widespread belief in and fear of the standardization of foods and food products across cultures. On the contrary, at Nestlé the expectation is that a growing number of market segments will develop, both horizontally, based on tradition, and vertically, based on age, lifestyle, and so on.

There are some foods that are sold in almost every country on the globe, such as the offerings of Coca-Cola and McDonald's. These do represent a global market segment. Although they are highly visible, however, they are the exception to the rule. Most food continues to be of a regional or even local nature. What globalization does for the regional and local consumer is to offer greater freedom of choice and an enhanced decision-making process. This means that within the confines of the consumer habits of a particular country, a person still experiences greater variety. In the food industry in particular, the priorities of consumers continue to lead to greater differentiation, not to homogeneity.

11

Nestlé in the Philippines

NESTLÉ'S SELF-IMAGE AND the perception others have of it vary from country to country. In certain places, notably in the West, Nestlé is frequently mentioned in connection with sensitive subjects such as globalization, the role of multinationals, and nutritional crises. In articles about Nestlé, "profit" sometimes becomes a synonym for "exploitation," "inside growth" morphs into "job deconstruction," and "higher demand" comes to means "manipulation through advertising."

Yet in other parts of the world the media deal with Nestlé mostly in a positive context, for example in small, regional announcements, or with respect to miscellaneous matters such as its sponsorship of cultural or sporting events.

In reality, there is very little difference between Nestlé plants and policies worldwide. With hardly any other company will one be referred with such frequency to company-wide principles that govern everyday business activities. Since, in the research for this book, the impressions received of Nestlé's operations and philosophy were on the whole positive, it seems to be the case that people in industrialized countries need to become aware that their opinions are not necessarily shared by the rest of the world. This is clearly the case in the Philippines, where Nestlé's operations provide a useful counterpoint to critics who perceive the company mostly in terms of exploitation.

First, some basics about the country. The Philippines is located south of Taiwan and northwest of Indonesia, in the fastest-growing region of Southeast Asia. The country comprises 300,000 square kilometers and consists of an archipelago of 7,107 islands. Sixty percent of its 75 million inhabitants live on the two main islands, Luzon and Mindanao. The capital, Manila, is on Luzon, and is composed of numerous incorporated suburbs and small municipalities. About 11 million people live there. The City of Davao, in the south of the island of Mindanao, covers a larger area but has only one million inhabitants.

The Filipinos are a young people, with an average age of just twenty-five. Since in the Philippines it is still customary for a family to have eight to ten children, more than half the population is under twenty. In 1998 annual population growth was calculated to be 1.7 million. That placed the Philippines in tenth position in terms of speed of population growth. First place is held by India, which adds 18.3 million people per year; China is next, with 12.5 million. The populations of Pakistan, Nigeria, and Indonesia, in that order, grow by three to five million every year. The United States is in sixth place, followed by Brazil, Bangladesh, and

Mexico, each of which increases its population annually by something over two million.

Children get good schooling in the Philippines. Since instruction takes place mainly in English, children grow up bilingual in English and Filipino. Schools are free and attendance mandatory between the ages of seven and twelve. One million young people are attending universities and colleges.

Since Filipinos speak good English, they have far greater flexibility in the job market after they complete school than the average European graduate. They often go abroad to study, choosing universities in the U.S., Australia, other Asian countries, or Europe. Filipinos are also found working abroad far more frequently than citizens of any other country. From wherever they are working, Filipinos usually send a large part of their foreign earnings home to their family. These returned earnings represent an annual influx into the economy of more than $10 billion.

Frequently, it is the women who support their families. In general, women in the Philippines are far more emancipated and their position much stronger than would at first glance appear to be the case. It is certainly not what a visitor familiar with other Asian countries would expect. Since 90 percent of all Filipinos are Catholic, their general outlook is similar to that of Western countries, and they fit into global society more easily than other Asians. Their command of English, their good education, and their willingness to leave home to find work make Filipinos ideal global citizens. Such committed and motivated workers are not easily found anywhere else in the world.

On our visit to the Philippines we had the opportunity to meet numerous women who have knowledge in areas that are repeatedly touched on by American and European critics of Nestlé.

Lilia Bautista receives us in the late afternoon, squeezing the interview between two meetings she is scheduled to attend. She has recently been appointed chairperson of the watchdog commission that oversees the Manila stock exchange. Increasingly, women are appointed to important official positions because they are better educated and able to take stronger action than men. This unexpected female power is due to the fact that men are frequently enmeshed in the "old boy's network," which tends to tie their hands.

Half of Filipino women are employed outside the home. However, their chances of advancing to leading positions are limited to the public sector, according to Mrs. Bautista. It is also true that the government pays women less than men in equivalent jobs. This is why many female teachers prefer factory jobs in semiconductor plants. Discrimination against women is by no means a thing of the past in the Philippines.

In the areas of public administration and legislation, Filipinos have modeled their country on the United States. A vast array of laws and regulations interlace the fabric of civil life. In response, a population conscious of its rights has ensured that there are more lawyers per capita in the Philippines than in any other place on earth. Business is the frequent target of the Filipino penchant for lawsuits. Foreigners are warned to start businesses only in the well-established sectors of the economy, where the most common bones of contention have already been sorted out.

Before Mrs. Bautista was put in charge of supervising the stock exchange, she was assistant secretary of state at the Ministry for Commerce and Industry, and in that capacity she represented the Philippines at various important international meetings. Still earlier, Mrs. Bautista, who is a lawyer by training, served as the Filipino consul in Geneva, Switzerland. Her career has made her familiar with Europe and has given her experience working with powerful people from around the world. Mrs. Bautista holds all significant economic data about her country in her head and quotes figures with great fluidity.

The gross national product of the Philippines increased by 2.5 percent in 1999, and an increase of 3.5 percent is expected for 2000. Gross domestic production went up 2 percent in 1999, and is expected to go up by 3 percent in 2000. The inflation rate for 2000 is predicted to be a light 6.7 to 7 percent.

Mrs. Bautista thinks that stable growth is very important. If the economy grows too fast, the danger of a recession increases. Forty percent of the population is still working in agriculture. The Asian Crisis of 1998 was weathered relatively well by the Philippines—better than by most other Asian countries. Having said that, the Philippines has a negative trade balance, that is to say, more goods are imported than exported.

Mrs. Bautista is of the opinion that, on the whole, the Philippines is in a fairly good economic position but is strongly underestimated abroad. High on the list of current governmental priorities is support for those industries that are based on agriculture. In this context, food processing and gene technology are seen as necessary if the country is to continue to sustain a growing population at home as well as have a chance of increasing its food exports.

Mrs. Bautista makes it very clear that foreign investors are welcome; their money is needed. Indeed, Nestlé is very much appreciated in the Philippines. The country has a large pool of well-trained labor, and foreign companies pay better than domestic ones. Mrs. Bautista is aware that Filipino women have a good reputation around the world as doctors, nurses, and domestic workers. She anticipates that the trend to employ them will continue globally, and she welcomes the opportunities this offers.

Ludivina Y. Garces-Holst is a physician, married to a Swede, which explains her unusual second surname. Everyone respectfully calls her "dottora." Her specialty is pediatrics, particularly pediatric endocrinology. She has several other responsibilities, one of them as a member of the American Board of Pediatrics. She sees patients on a rotating schedule in three different medical centers. Several important developments in the treatment of sick children in the Philippines are credited to Dr. Garces-Holst.

Dr. Garces is a lively, petite woman who does not mince words. As a venue for our interview she has chosen the venerable Polo Club of Manila, of which she is of course a member. The historic wooden structure with its broad roofs, surrounded by gardens and the green expanses of the polo grounds, is located in the center of modern Manila. No one would dream of putting this large piece of prime real estate to any use more relevant than polo.

Dr. Garces considers it important that foreigners understand the special problems as well as the special advantages of the Filipino lifestyle. It is part of the emancipation of women that they are employed and able to work outside the home. This only becomes a problem when the mother is expected to breast-feed her baby consistently. It is impossible for most mothers to return home during their lunch hour, breast-feed their baby, and then return to work on time; distances tend to be enormous, even within the city, and transportation can be slow. Dr. Garces finds that nowadays women prefer to use a good baby formula to bottle-feed their infants. She mentions how people in Europe were outraged by this change, but as a doctor she finds it unobjectionable.

Dr. Garces adds that no one has the right to question the economic decisions of women or to curb their independence. She adds that, in her experience, respect for self-determination is stronger in the Philippines than in Europe. She finds this to be particularly true in the area of medicine.

Alice Sanz de la Gente has been president of the Association of Filipino Midwives since 1987, and from 1996 to 1999 she was also president of the International Midwives' Society, the ICM. It happens that in 1999 the international convention of midwives, attended by a thousand practitioners, met in Manila. Considering how distinguished a woman Alice Sanz de la Gente is, her office is remarkably modest.

The Association of Filipino Midwives has pursued the same goals for many years through its four-pronged campaign: anti-abortion, promotion of breast-feeding, birth control, and cancer prevention. Nestlé supports these aims in the context of a public–private–partnership.

Over the years, Nestlé's activities on behalf of the Association of Midwives have been wide-ranging. Nestlé shoulders the costs of running their office, finances courses on baby care for mothers, and supports the association's efforts to improve the training of midwives. The corporation has also made possible Ms. de la Gente's participation in international congresses. Ms. de la Gente says that she has never been asked by Nestlé to recommend Nestlé products.

In the past, midwifery was not a recognized profession in the Philippines. It took years of fighting before Ms. de la Gente was able to achieve a reasonable and officially recognized level of training for midwives. Today, 147,000 midwives are active throughout the Islands. They play an especially important role in the countryside.

The guidance and advice offered by midwives extends far beyond matters obstetrical and nutritional. Sometimes they have to replace the doctor; at other times they are expected to settle family problems or even disputes between neighbors. The midwife is often the only independent person that villagers can talk to, and of course they all know her.

Alice Sanz de la Gente is very clear in saying that

without the support of Nestlé, she would not have been able to make such important changes, either in the education of midwives or in reducing the rate of infant mortality.

Clearly, the women we interviewed do not share the point of view of Nestlé's Western critics. Their attitude is pragmatic and fact-based, and they have no bones to pick with Nestlé. Nor are their views inspired by ideology; they are based on actual successes in particular fields.

Manila is not a romantic city. There is no city center like the ones we know in Paris, London, New York, or most other Western cities. Manila consists of many centers, which in turn are broken up into still smaller units. The most expensive and luxurious neighborhoods—where the trees are tall and venerable, and the villas boast a degree of magnificence not often found even in the United States and Europe—are a mere stone's throw away from huddles of miserable huts hammered together of wood and corrugated iron.

No city in east Asia operates under the elaborate and strict environmental regulations that Manila has, yet the atmosphere could not be worse. Endless lines of idling cars stuck in traffic jams emit exhaust fumes from five in the morning till deep into the night.

The Nestlé Center, which was opened in 1999, is located in Makati City. In this part of Manila, gleaming new hotels and commercial buildings reach skywards—cheek by jowl with one- and two-story homes. The Nestlé Center is an architecturally modest and functional structure, as are all of the corporation's buildings around the world. One special feature is the electronic elevator. You have to press the usual buttons to let it know your floor, but in addition you have tell it how many people it has to take where, so that it never keeps anyone waiting for long.

One thing that strikes you when you visit the Manila Nestlé Center is its simplicity, not to say sparseness. In this respect it is no different than Nestlé headquarters in Switzerland or any other Nestlé building anywhere in the world. Hardly any pictures adorn the walls. Only at the entrance to the meeting rooms is there one, which serves as a symbol of the Filipino nation. It shows a group of people moving the house of a neighbor. This sense of union based on co-operation is basic to the Filipino outlook.

On the lower floor of the building there is a glass-enclosed store. Here employees can buy all Nestlé products that are available in their country. At the same time the store serves as a showroom, displaying all that is being offered. It is visited by numerous groups of all kinds, starting with the women who use the Nestlé cooking studio.

This company store could be in any country in the world except that—on closer inspection—you find that the writing on the packages is in a foreign language and the pictures show some unknown products. But otherwise anyone would feel right at home, seeing Nescafé, Maggi, and other global brands. Apart from the text (which is in a mixture of English and Filipino) you would recognize all the packaging, because it is the same in color and layout as what you are used to seeing at home, wherever you happen to live.

Filipino consumers pay a lot more attention to health factors in choosing their foods than most people do in Europe or North America. For this reason the ingredients and the healthful aspects of a product are prominently integrated into its image, both on the package and in terms of its promotion.

Consumers in the West use different criteria when they shop for food. They are interested primarily in the taste sensations they can expect, and they want to have a lot of information about how the product is going to perform when it is prepared or served. Filipino cooks, in contrast, put their trust in their own skills. Generally speaking, Western consumers want to know what results to expect from the food once it is on the plate. In the Philippines the consumer wants to know about the quality of the product.

Every package displays the Nestlé nest, and even the two-gram envelope of Nescafé Classic shows the Web address and telephone number of the Nestlé Consumer Service in Manila. Anyone with a question or comment can reach Nestlé by phone or over the Internet. The package also displays the admonition "Keep the Philippines Beautiful," a reminder not to throw the wrapping away on the street but to put it in a wastebasket. Of course, in Western countries the injunction would be to recycle it, but as yet there is no recycling system in the Philippines.

One feature of every Nestlé Center is the generous employee cafeteria, where reasonably priced foods are served all day long. Another place that is never missing is the Mother and Child Room, where mothers can breast-feed their babies during working hours, should they wish to do so. Such rooms exist in all Nestlé plants around the world. They are the corporation's way of demonstrating their willingness to support breast-feeding, where it makes sense and where it is in the company's power to make it possible.

The baby-food action groups, not surprisingly, consider this policy pure propaganda. They see it as a form of provocation that, of all multinational companies, it should be Nestlé that complies with their explicit demand for this service. They react as if it annoys them. Perhaps this is another indication that the whole campaign is absurd.

The president of Nestlé Philippines, Inc. is Juan B. Santos. His career is typical for a Nestlé manager. After training at the Citibank, he went on to study in the U.S. He was then employed for a while by Coca-Cola in the Philippines, before coming to Nestlé in 1964. As a product assistant at Nestlé he worked in various areas. He was then chosen to be part of the International Management Development Program, and in 1972 he went to Lausanne, Switzerland, for training.

An important milestone in Santos's career came at the end of the 1970s, when he was transferred to the head office in Vevey to become familiar with Nestlé's worldwide management methods. In 1985 he was put in charge of Nestlé's activities in Thailand, only to return to the Philippines in 1987 to take on the posts of chairman and CEO of Nestlé Philippines, Inc.

Between 1991 and 1996, Santos was working both at home and in Singapore, where he acted as negotiator for the ASEAN (Association of Southeast Asian Nations) Industrial Joint Venture Program. Apart from the automobile industry, Nestlé is the only business to have an independent agreement with the ASEAN nations. Through this agreement, customs charges for Nestlé products have been reduced by as much as 90 percent across the entire ASEAN region. This has made it possible for Nestlé to centralize its production for the Asian arena. Thus, chocolate is produced in Malaysia for the whole of Asia, Singapore is the center for soy sauce, the Philippines for breakfast cereals, and Thailand for coffee creamer.

Santos is the kind of leader who is appreciated at Nestlé. He is both a visionary and a pragmatist; he thinks long term but can act fast to implement his plans. He is experienced and open to new ideas, careful and courageous. You can feel his energy and the will to achieve, though these qualities are combined in him with great friendliness and patience.

Santos leads his team with restraint, but with assuredness as well. His staff consists of both Filipinos and so-called expatriates—pre-eminent visiting members of the international management team. You can see that for Santos, the human being is always central, whether as a customer, a supplier, or an employee. He never seems to lose sight of the social context, while also keeping an eye on his markets. His aim is to offer the best possible products at the lowest possible price.

Asked about his particular formula for success, Juan

Santos, who is known as "the Boss," lists five points. The first three come as no surprise. First: good, consistent, and long-term communications about brands. Second: tight management, involving a team where young employees and experienced veterans work together. Third: a highly motivated workforce, which is not an unusual aim but which is reflected here in many unusual management practices.

Even in the south of the Islands, where development has not yet made many inroads, there are Nestlé employees with European training and people who gained some of their work experience abroad. In a developed country, no corporation would consider giving international management training to a local employee who works in the field, visiting small dealers or putting up little advertisements on market stalls. This would be seen as a waste of training. At Nestlé, it is regarded as an investment in the future, and the sales figures bear this out.

Santos makes use of the special Philippine custom of wearing corporate uniforms to increase identification with the employer. In accordance with tradition, the company pays for the uniforms. At Nestlé, management attire is also made to serve as a uniform, and there are elaborate rules on what to wear each day: Mondays, gray pants with a blue shirt and black tie; Tuesdays, blue pants and a white shirt; and so on. Such regulations also exist for the female office staff, of course. These rules are posted in all Nestlé enterprises in the Philippines, and right next to them are the management principles of Helmut Maucher.

Somewhat surprising is the fourth of Santos's five rules

for success: small package size. In the Philippines, 70 percent of Nestlé's sales involve small units of 25 or 50 grams. For one cup of Nescafé you need two grams. It follows, then, that the popular 25- and 50-gram packages of Nescafé provide twelve to twenty-five cups. For the average Philippine household this represents only one or two days' supply. Serving coffee is far more than just a courtesy to guests; for Filipinos it is an absolute requirement in every social situation. The national preference for small packages also applies to milk powder. The so-called soft packs, containing 80 or 200 grams, represent 85 percent of sales.

Santos's fifth rule of success is maintaining a high profile at the point of sale. In small local markets you will be led by rows of small flags to the stands that carry certain Nestlé brands, such as Maggi products or soup bases. In supermarkets too, advertising and the clear presence of Nestlé brands is considered very important.

Managers like Santos are only one reason why Nestlé continues to attract local talent. Of Nestlé's 4,900 employees in the Philippines, 43 percent have university or high school diplomas; 26 percent have completed various types of professional training; and another 26 percent have degrees from some other school of higher learning. The majority of the employees are between twenty-six and forty-five years of age.

A worker at Nestlé earns on average about 619 pesos per day. Industry-wide, the average is only 446 pesos, while the country's legal minimum wage is set at 223 pesos. In addition to their salaries, Nestlé workers receive other incomes and benefits, which amount on average to an extra 506 pesos per day per Nestlé employee. The average daily earnings of an employee at Nestlé therefore add up to 1,125 pesos, or about $27.50. This is well above the industry average of 811 pesos ($19.85), and far above the total minimum wage of 360 pesos ($8.82 dollars).

The benefits of Nestlé workers include life insurance and a bonus of a thirteenth or even a fourteenth monthly salary in a year. In the case of an employee falling ill, the company covers 75 percent of the cost of treatments for the worker, and extends the same benefits to members of her family.

Other extras include a sack of rice per month, rent support, and special assistance in case of death, for the employee and his family. In the company store, employees can shop at a discount, and during their coffee and lunch breaks they can consume Nestlé products without charge. Gift packages at Christmas time and on the occasion of the worker's birthday also count among the perks.

All Nestlé pension monies are invested in independently managed funds. Employees who leave the company can choose between a pension and a one-time payment. Ninety percent of employees choose the latter, and use the money to buy or build a house. Nestlé also offers courses in how to manage money.

Nestlé tries to maintain maximum transparency for the benefit of its employees and customers, and anyone else who is interested. Numerous brochures are produced, an official monthly newsletter called *Abenta* and the bi-weekly *Nestl Family Balita*, a very detailed report on company activities that is also sent to Filipinos working in Nestlé installations abroad.

Training receives high priority at Nestlé Philippines. In 1999 a total of 22 million pesos—15 percent of personnel costs—was spent on training. Nestlé offers a wide range of courses, relating both to work functions and to personal development. In addition to training in management, leadership, and team building, there are many specific professional training opportunities.

In all Nestlé plants in the Philippines, each worker is expected to make a personal contribution to the success of the enterprise as a whole. To this end, the company organizes Small Group Activities and Quality Circles. The purpose of these groups is to identify possible projects to improve the production process in the group's area, to analyze problems, and to work out solutions. Each change may make only a very small difference, but the total effect of all these activities is to noticeably enhance production and lower production costs.

Nestlé Philippines also maintains many social and sports activities, from chess to basketball. Over and above that, Nestlé offers sports vacations for workers' entire families, as well as activities for the children of working parents. Within the general framework of a scholarship program in force since 1996, Nestlé also identifies employees' particularly gifted children and supports them throughout their education.

Another thing that will strike the informed visitor to any of Nestlé Philippines' factories is how the Japanese principle of *kaizen*, or continuous improvement, is rigorously applied. *Kaizen* is based on the notion that many small improvements will create and maintain a steady stream of progress. In North America and in Europe, corporate managers often struggle with the *kaizen* system, mostly because it requires leadership that is transparent and that shares information with employees.

Nestlé's role in the Philippines has not always been so proactive. It started its activities there in 1895, and in 1899 opened its first import distribution center. During World War II the company was forced to end all commercial activities in the Philippines. Yet soon after the war a new beginning was made. Under the name Filipro Inc., the corporation was able once again to import Milo, Nido milk powder, Milkmaid condensed milk, and Nescafé.

In the 1950s the government of the Philippines introduced import controls, so Nestlé was practically forced to begin the construction of its own production facilities. In 1960, Nestlé SA joined forces with a large Filipino concern, San Miguel Corp., to create Joint Venture Nutripro, Inc. The purpose of this business venture was to produce food. Two years later its first facility, the Alabang factory, began operations.

In 1977, Filipro and Nutripro, the Nestlé trading and production companies, merged to form a new entity. This was at first called Filipor, Inc., but was renamed Nestlé Philippines Inc. in 1986. At the Alabang factory, only coffee was made at first, but later condensed milk was produced under the brand names Milkmaid, Carnation, Alpine, and Bear Brand.

Today, Nestlé Philippines owns six factories, which produce Nestlé brand foods for the local market and breakfast cereals for export. The assumption, often repeated, that Nestlé supplies the whole world from its European factories turns out to be wrong. To produce its goods Nestlé chooses those sites where production is most feasible, and where anticipated future developments justify investment.

This is by no means the policy of all food-producing companies. In Davao, in the southern part of the Philippines, there is a large supermarket where you can buy cold orange juice that was bottled in Denmark. Oranges do not grow in Denmark. You can imagine the high markup and profit margins achieved in transporting a tropical beverage from its source in one hot country to another via Scandinavia.

Nestlé's second factory was built in Cabuyao in 1976. It manufactures Milo drinks, Nido and Bear Brand milk powder, baby food, prepared foods, and culinary products.

The third Nestlé factory is located in the north of Mindanao, ten kilometers east of Cagayan de Oro, "the city of golden friendship." The Cagayan de Oro factory is a good example of how Nestlé operates. Of the employees at this factory, 67 percent are between twenty-five and thirty-five years of age; another 30 percent are between thirty-five and forty-five. Thirty-five percent are college graduates, while 26 percent have technical training. Employees participate in many workers' groups and special teams, over and above their jobs. There is a first-aid group, a voluntary fire brigade, a security committee, a hygiene task force, and an environmental task force.

Built in 1984, the factory today concentrates on two product lines, coffee and milk products, both of which are made by the same spray-drying process. This is in itself a fascinating procedure.

To make Nescafé, green coffee beans are first cleaned and then roasted and ground. After that, the coffee is brewed by a special process with hot water, in what amounts to a huge coffee machine. The filtered and highly concentrated coffee is then fed into the top of a spray tower. A nozzle in the summit then sprays the liquid under high pressure. Hot air causes the liquid component of the coffee concentrate to evaporate, so that by the time it reaches the bottom of the tower, it is a powder: soluble, dry coffee. This powdered coffee is further refined before it is finally packaged.

With dried milk products the process is very similar. Raw milk powder from Australia is mixed with water, pasteurized with steam, and enriched with product-specific nutrients. It is then spray-dried, very much like Nescafé, in a tower called an Egron. After the powder has cooled, it can be packaged.

In the Philippines, as elsewhere, cleanliness is the most important characteristic of a food production plant. For this reason, at Nestlé plants, visitors cannot enter sensitive areas, even if they are wearing protective clothing.

The production process itself takes place in an almost completely sealed space. At the beginning of the process you can see the raw material; at the very end you see the packaged product. On such a sealed production line it would be impossible for workers to drop things into vats or for foreign objects to be processed along with the food.

In its external landscaping and maintenance, Nestlé makes sure to reflect the same principles that govern its internal operations. The grounds of all Nestlé factories are oversized, well-maintained, green landscapes. The buildings are always freshly painted, the walkways recently swept. If a piece of wood falls off a passing truck, someone comes and picks it up.

In the Philippines, any Nestlé building is easily distinguishable from the competition's plants. Who would want to drink the milk made by the Alaska Milk Company, when their very name is peeling off the walls and the building is squeezed between others in a gray industrial complex near Manila?

Nestlé also strives to make its factories eco-friendly. The environment is a special concern of Rudy P. Trillanes, the head of operations at Cagayan de Oro. Coffee grounds are burned in a special oven to produce heat for the factory. All liquid waste is thoroughly cleaned so that it can be used to water the factory grounds.

An extra strip of land was purchased and added to the lot on which the factory stands because a big old tree was growing there. Only by including it in the property could Nestlé guarantee that the tree would not one day be sacrificed to widen some future highway. You could call it a gesture, or you could see it as a symbol. Either way, it is something the people of Cagayan de Oro remember.

Another aspect of the environmental protection program at the factory is the system for recycling the heat given off during the process of production. Thus, in the commercial production of food, nothing needs to be wasted; everything can be used. In this respect, commercially produced food can actually be more environmentally friendly than home-cooked meals. Few people understand that commercial food producers can be both economically and ecologically more efficient than any private household ever has the means to be.

Nestlé also looks to support microbusinesses. Consider its ice-cream venture. Since 1996 its Philippine factory has been producing ice cream in commercial-sized packages. Frozen novelties and chilled foods are also produced, including yogurt and Chamyto, a mini-beverage with probiotics. Ice-cream consumption in the Philippines has always been fairly low, at only 0.7 liters per person per year. The reason for this is that there are still relatively few homes that boast a refrigerator. To boost ice-cream consumption, and to help street peddlers make a living, Nestlé has been providing them with small freezer bins.

Since 1998, Nestlé SA of Vevey, Switzerland, has owned 100 percent of Nestlé Philippines. One of the largest enterprises in the Philippines, Nestlé is in eleventh position, with sales of 35,035 billion pesos. It is the largest foreign corporation, ahead of Coca-Cola Bottlers, which has sales of 28,969 billion pesos (all 1998 figures). Within the area of food and beverages, only the indigenous San Miguel Corporation is larger than Nestlé, with sales of 78,226 billion pesos. For Nestlé, the Philippines operation counts among its thirteen most important markets. From 1997 to 2000 the company experienced an average annual growth rate of 10 percent.

Nestlé's growth in the Philippines comes despite the fact that government regulations tend to keep prices down. The reason for this is that, whenever inflation in the Philippines grows beyond a certain level, the state intervenes, using price controls. When this happens, goods must be sold at a given price. Accordingly, annual net profits have fluctuated between plus 66 percent in 1992 and minus 5.7 percent in 1998. In 1999 net profits rose by 13.6 percent, or 8.0 percent of sales. For 2000 a powerful surge in profits is equivalent to 9.5 percent of sales.

Nestlé invests heavily in the Philippines. Between 1991 and 1998 annual spending on physical plants and immaterial business assets totaled between 4.2 and 8.2 percent of proceeds. In 1999 this figure stood at 4.0 percent, and in 2000 it was expected to be 4.2 percent. These are extremely high rates of annual investment compared with the average overall reinvestment of Nestlé, which is around 4 percent of global proceeds.

The extent to which Nestlé invests in the Philippines is matched by its efforts to market its products locally. Milk and beverages account for 80 percent of Nestlé Philippines' business. The rest comprises prepared foods, ice cream, sweets, and products for the food service industry. Seven hundred employees work in the marketing area, four hundred of them in sales. Marketing is broken up first into product groups and then into individual products.

The product groups for marketing purposes are Milk Products, Coffee and Beverages, Infant Foods, Prepared Foods, and Food Service Products. There are also a variety of very small product groups, such as Clinical Foods, Breakfast Cereals, and Pet Foods, which have little significance in the overall Philippine sales picture.

In terms of business volume, the picture looks like this:

Product Name	Amount Sold (metric tons)	
	1987	1999
Nescafé	3,600	17,000
Milo beverages	6,500	28,000
Nestea	300	5,000
Nestlé Bear Brand	16,000	50,000
Nido milk powder	8,500	23,000
Coffee-mate	1,000	11,000

In the case of all these products Nestlé is the market leader within each of the market segments concerned. The company has a commanding lead in sales of instant coffee and coffee whitener, supplying 90 percent of the market, and it also dominates sales of condensed milk, with 74 percent of all Philippine sales.

Analyzing the market more closely, one finds that the traditional retail channels constitute 80 percent of all outlets, but in terms of sales volume they account for only 53 percent of total business. Among the traditional channels are the local grocery stores. There are 4,527 of these on all the Philippine islands. For Nestlé they produce 36 percent of total sales. There are also 2,670 market stalls, which are located in the so-called "wet markets." These markets, also called Sari Sari, account for only 9 percent of total sales volume. This happens to be the same proportion as the total sales produced by the 337 food wholesalers.

The wet markets play a special role in developing brand loyalty. They are called wet because much of what is offered for sale there is fresh ("wet") food. This is where day laborers do their daily food shopping, as do other people who cannot afford or do not wish to invest in a refrigerator.

Shopping every day means buying in small quantities. This is the traditional way, especially in rural areas, where only about half of the population has access to a fridge. Wholesalers supply many small businesses, which in turn visit the most remote mountain villages with their pickup trucks.

There are also 456 supermarkets in the Philippines, and they represent the new way and the way of the future. This small number of outlets is responsible for 28 percent of Nestlé's total sales. About the same volume of business is produced by 478 mini-marts. Drugstores and convenience stores make up about 5 percent more. Gasoline stations, which have become a very significant part of Nestlé's distribution system in industrialized countries, bring in only 0.1% of total sales in the Philippines.

In the south of the Philippines, Carnation, the brand that Nestlé took over 17 years ago, is well known and well loved. For this reason the Carnation packages are still on the supermarket shelves in that region, although the content of the Carnation and Nestlé packages is in every way identical.

In the Philippines, as elsewhere, Nestlé is always introducing new brands. One of these is the ready-to-drink Milo Tonic Food-Drink, which is sold in small plastic bottles. Another is Neslac Children's Milk Powder, enriched with Bifidus or Chamyto, a lactobacillus culture that corresponds to the LC1 yogurt sold in Europe. While LC1 GO is aimed at health-conscious adults, Chamyto was created for children. Ready-to-eat rice dishes by Maggi, which require only heating, have also opened a completely new market segment in the Islands.

New flavors have to be added constantly to keep up with changing consumer tastes. For example, Nestlé has invented a cheese ice cream, which contains, not cream cheese, but chunks of cheddar. Another variety contains small toys.

Maintaining healthy markets also means that older products have to be refreshed. Enriching Nido milk powder with protein, calcium, and zinc to promote growth, is an example of this process. Bear Brand milk powder has been similarly upgraded. In marketing nutritional products, the issues of calcium and osteoporosis play a part here as elsewhere. You can buy Nestlé Carnation with extra calcium, and the Philippine Osteoporosis Association supports this product on its Web site.

On the pop culture side, Nestlé is targeting the same market as McDonald's and Pizza Hut. Nestea has now become a part of fast food restaurant fare. Nestea machines are also installed in schools, and automats dispensing Nescafé are becoming more common. These dispensers target mostly young consumers. The message is clear: Nescafé coffee should not be confined to breakfast at home; it should be enjoyed in public as well. Nor does it always have to be consumed hot.

Coffee is a commodity like no other on the Philippine Islands. It is not just that it is consumed on every possible occasion and that "coffee" almost always means Nescafé; the production of coffee is also a very special thing.

For most people in the developed countries, coffee has become a sort of staple food—a regular component of breakfast and a steady companion during the working day. No one thinks much about it, as long as it is hot and tastes reasonably good.

The kick in coffee—as everyone knows—is caused by the caffeine it contains. Caffeine is a potentially dangerous substance in that it is both stimulating and addictive. It is the combination of the stimulating effect, the wonderful aroma, and the fine taste that make coffee a popular beverage around the world.

Chemically speaking, caffeine is an alkaloid, specifically

one of the xanthines, which occur not only in coffee beans but also in tea leaves, coca beans, and other plants. The average cup of coffee contains 80 to 150 milligrams of caffeine. By comparison, a can of Coke contains 30 to 50 milligrams. Although 100 grams of tea leaves contains more caffeine than the equivalent weight of coffee, a cup of tea is lower in caffeine than a cup of coffee, as it takes much less tea than coffee to brew one cup.

How much caffeine will be served in a cup of coffee depends on several factors: the type of coffee bean used, how the beans are roasted, how fine they are ground, and the method of brewing. Although dark-roasted coffees have a more powerful aroma, they actually contain less caffeine than lighter roasts, since the longer roasting time destroys more of it. The amount of caffeine given off by the beans is also directly related to how finely they are ground: the finer the grind, the more caffeine in the brew.

Caffeine unfolds its full effect within thirty to sixty minutes of consumption. Via various biochemical processes, it stimulates brain activity. Two cups of coffee are sufficient to affect an EEG, which shows the increased brain activity. Four or five cups will increase heart rate and breathing. Caffeine accelerates all important bodily functions: breathing, heartbeat, and digestion. It also alleviates fatigue, sharpens concentration, and speeds mental processes.

Too much caffeine causes irritability, nervousness, overexcitement, or even diarrhea. Caffeine addicts need a regular fix to combat tiredness and headaches, and to increase their concentration. Giving up the caffeine habit can be difficult, and in some cases can even be accompanied by withdrawal symptoms.

On the positive side, coffee consumption seems to be related to a lower suicide rate; drinking at least two cups a day lowers the level of irritation and raises spirits. Coffee is also said to enhance social skills, increase self-confidence, and boost energy levels. It seems that moderate coffee drinkers suffer less often from high blood pressure and diabetes. They also have been found to take fewer mood-altering drugs and less medication for gastric ulcers, anxiety attacks, and high blood pressure.

The coffee break at the office does more than recharge employees' batteries. The social component of this ritual is actually far more important. Over a good cup of coffee, people will relax, talk, and kid around. This helps many employees get through a long, tiring workday.

Critics of coffee claim that society conceals the dangers of caffeine by stressing the beverage's social appeal, and in this way offers a fertile field for the marketing campaigns of the coffee business. Critics cite coffee ads as proof of their position. The ads never address the pharmacological aspects of the beverage. Instead, they concentrate on harmonious family scenes, leisure-time activities, and the simple enjoyment of the aroma and the taste. Furthermore, say the critics of coffee, those who sell it have always taken a lively interest in the coffee break, and they support this habit as an important ritual through their advertisements and by providing special office coffee-service products.

All of this may be true. Still, the critics might do well to look at the alternative to the coffee break: a world without enjoyment and of lessened quality.

In the Philippines, coffee also plays an important role as a crop. The two most important species of coffee grown today are Arabica, which thrives in mountainous regions and accounts for 75 percent of total world production, and Canephora, better known as Robusta. This is generally a more resistant strain; it is also a more generous producer, contains more caffeine, and needs a tropical climate to grow. Today, more and more hybrids of the two species are being planted. Total world coffee production is at six million metric tons. Of this, Nestlé buys 720,000 metric tons, or about 12 percent. This makes Nestlé the largest buyer of green coffee.

The main growers of Arabica are Brazil, Colombia, Mexico, and Guatemala. Robasta is planted in Brazil, Vietnam, Indonesia, India, and the Ivory Coast. The five main importers of coffee are the U.S., Germany, France, Japan, and Great Britain. The economic importance of coffee in global terms can be appreciated from the fact that— after crude oil—it is the second most important commodity on world markets.

The coffee plant was introduced to the Philippines in the eighteenth century. Today, 30,000 farms grow coffee, and 95 percent of these are small farms. Annual coffee consumption within the country is about 50,000 metric tons. Of this, Nestlé processed 43,500 metric tons in 1999. When necessary, coffee is imported from Indonesia or Vietnam.

Although the acreage under coffee in the Philippines has not changed since 1998, remaining a constant 112,500 hectares, the coffee yield fluctuates considerably. In 1998 the total harvest was at 37,000 metric tons, in 1999, it rose to 44,000 metric tons, and in 2000 it fell back to 34,000 metric tons. There was a corresponding ebb and flow in the amount of coffee Nestlé could buy in each of those three years: 30,000, 37,000, and 27,000 metric tons respectively.

The price of coffee is an important consideration in looking at these figures. In 1998 the world market price of coffee averaged 67 Philippine pesos per kilogram. Nestlé paid 65 pesos domestically but had to pay 94 pesos for imported beans. The situation had changed dramatically by 1999. The world price had fallen to 50 pesos; Nestlé bought domestic coffee at a higher price, namely 56.5 pesos. For imported coffee the corporation had to pay only slightly more, 59 pesos. In the spring of 2000 the world price of Philippine coffee had fallen to 35 pesos per kilo. Domestically, Nestlé paid almost a quarter more, 43.88 pesos, just below the price of imported coffee, which was then at 44.37 pesos.

These numbers demonstrate Nestlé's policy of support-ing domestic coffee growers. Paying higher prices, however, is not all the corporation does. Nestlé also maintains an agricultural technical assistance service in the Philippines. Since 1962 the main concern of this office has been coffee. The assistance service's aim is twofold: to improve the yield of the coffee farms and to raise the quality of the beans. At this time 55 percent of all coffee shrubs on the Islands are over twenty years old. It is necessary to think about replacing them, and at the same time about improving the way the coffee "berry" is handled after it is harvested.

With these aims in mind Nestlé has started a research and demonstration farm in Tagum, about sixty kilometers outside Davao, in the far south of the island of Mindanao. The farm offers training programs for coffee farmers. In 1999 a total of thirteen thousand persons were instructed there in the details of coffee growing. It is Nestlé's hope to stop the ongoing decline of the Philippine coffee crop. On a well-maintained coffee ranch, yields of 2.5 to 4.0 metric tons per hectare are completely realistic. By comparison, the current average crop of Philippine coffee plantations varies between 250 and 900 kilograms per hectare. Experts call the coffee grown in the Philippines "jungle coffee."

Vietnam is a good example of what can be achieved with well-aimed shifts in agricultural methods. Over six years beginning in 1990, the total yield of Vietnamese coffee plantations rose from 50,000 metric tons to 240,000 metric tons. By 1999 it had reached 375,000 metric tons, and it is expected to level out at around 700,000.

Looking into the causes of the decline in the Philippine coffee crop, it is strange not to be able to pin them down to the usual factors. The suspicion that the climate has changed is not borne out by the facts. Changes in the price of coffee do not offer an adequate reason either. Though the price per kilo has diminished by about 50 percent, the current level is still quite lucrative.

Nonetheless, the acreage under coffee is shrinking. In

1999 new planting added 850 hectares, but that same year 450 hectares went out of cultivation. The newly planted trees will start bearing in the year 2002, but as compared with 1999 the net increase will consist of only 400 hectares. Vietnam will have added 25,000 hectares by then.

With Filipino farmers, short-term goals are given the highest priority. Planting coffee is not of particular interest to them, and they are unwilling to invest in this commodity. This means that only the simplest equipment and insufficient labor are devoted to the coffee plantations, which in turn yields disappointing results. Profits are predictably modest. The outcome is a lack of interest in engaging in the cultivation of coffee.

One reason why long-term planning is unappealing is that small farmers in the Philippines are allowed to plant and harvest on public lands. Since the land is not theirs, however, they have little interest in making it profitable in the long run. The economics of profitable coffee cultivation encompass thirty or forty years of income, after money and time have been invested in the right way. As long as the farmers don't own the land, their attitude is not likely to change.

Other cash crops compete successfully with coffee on the Islands. In addition to being the number-one copra exporter in the world, the Philippines also grows a lot of sugar cane and rice, as well as some wheat. In the short run, all these crops bring relatively high returns as compared with coffee. Many small farmers also rely on government support, and as long as that is not forthcoming for coffee, they will always regard it as a secondary crop, and plant their coffee bushes under the coconut trees. Up to five years ago mangoes were profitable, because they require little work and there was government support for planting the trees. For this reason mango trees were preferred to coffee bushes.

The government likes to blame the industry for the whole situation, and many farmers do the same thing, as if they only planted coffee to please Nestlé. Yet it is precisely in coffee that Nestlé sees a real hope for the future of Philippine farmers. Although politically the most significant crop is rice, and many of the measures taken by the government are directed at rice production, coffee will maintain its primacy as a commodity.

Knowing this full well, Nestlé supports coffee farmers through its buying policy. Twelve depots have been established where farmers can deliver their coffee beans. The policies followed at these Nestlé stations are calculated to induce trust and produce a profit for the farmers. All prices are posted and compared with world rates. All suppliers are treated exactly the same. There is one standard for quality and price, and it is clearly displayed. All calculations are accurate, and what is particularly important, all payments are made instantly and in cash.

12

Pure or Processed?:
The Great Food Controversy

THE DEBATE OVER INDUSTRIALLY processed foods is one that engages industry experts, the media, and interest groups such as Friends of the Earth and Greenpeace. The opinions and agendas of these various players expose the complexity of the world in which Nestlé deals, a world that too often seems to trade in misinformation.

Are genetically modified crops the way to end world hunger or a new form of imperialism? Do today's food giants, such as Nestlé, think green or just think profits? And what does the public really think about processed foods?

To start with the last question, the average consumer's attitudes are contradictory. When questioned, few people express negative attitudes to industrially prepared foods, and even fewer intend to avoid them. That said, almost 96 percent of those questioned in one survey declared that a diet based on alternative, non-industrial foods is healthier, although fewer than 15 percent showed any interest in going that route.

In the same contradictory vein, a 2000 Swiss study, in which Nestlé participated, found that 82 percent of the population considered themselves well informed on the subject of nutrition, and 75 percent claimed that they watched what they ate—this despite the fact that fully one-third of all Swiss are overweight, another third never eat breakfast, and the amount of vegetables and fruit consumed in Switzerland is three times less than it would be if everyone regularly ate the recommended daily amounts.

The discrepancies point to some fascinating conclusions, the main one being that the majority of today's consumers are neither able to judge the quality of basic fresh ingredients nor use them very much. They also lack the culinary skills and the time required to prepare and preserve foods. And they refuse to accept the regional and seasonal limitations of an all-natural diet. These are some of the reasons why—contrary to apparent consumer preferences—80 to 90 percent of all the foods offered for sale undergo some industrial preparation.

Why, then, do so many people claim an attachment to natural foods? The simple reason is that, lacking basic knowledge of food ingredients and preparation, they rely on media sources whose penchant is to emphasize problems, scandals, and mistakes. In this climate it is not surprising that a gulf has opened up between the opinions consumers parrot second-hand from the media, on the one hand, and their actual food choices. Only this lack of intellectual congruity can explain why the sales of certain products and brands will soar despite widespread verbal rejection of same.

Media bias is also the reason why consumers and experts always seem to clash in their judgments about the risks involved in processed foods. Experts see the main danger to food in possible accidental contamination by bacteria that can spread diseases. They focus on various forms of "food poisoning," mostly intestinal complaints, which affect millions of people every year. Salmonella contained in eggs and meat is the main cause. This sort of disease can of course be averted by proper food preparation and storage, but such risks are not top of mind with most consumers. They see a far greater danger in food additives, a subject of only remote interest to the experts.

Things are much the same when it comes to allergies. According to the Webster of the International Food and Information Council, some five million Americans suffer from food allergies. Critics of industrial food like to blame this on dyes, preservatives and flavoring, but the overwhelming reason for these allergies is the foods themselves—usually grain proteins, eggs, peanuts, soybeans, milk and fish. Furthermore, one German study has shown that while the number of allergy sufferers overall has risen 30 to 40 percent in the last sixty years, food allergies account only for about 10 percent of this. The real reason for the increase, according to the German association of allergy specialists, is the growing population of household mites.

Television is one of the main culprits in spreading misleading information about food, often with a fair amount of theatricality. To cite just one example, on August 30, 2000, an episode in a German series entitled *What is Found in*

Our Food? posed as its question of the day: "How does saw-dust end up in [raspberry] yogurt?" The astonishing answer turned out to be that no sawdust is put into the yogurt at all, only a flavoring made from a natural product, cedar wood.

A more serious misrepresentation arose in connection with the bacterial strains that are added to Nestlé's LC1 yogurt and similar products. These are bacteria that occur naturally in the intestines, and are healthy for the body. A television program raised the question, "Where do these bacteria come from?" The answer was, "They come from feces. They are fecal bacteria." The accompanying pictures showed sewage plants, giving the viewer the impression that the food industry literally takes fecal matter, extracts certain components, and then processes these into food. The truth is that the bacteria are cultivated in laboratories, under strictly hygienic conditions.

Still another example of a confusing presentation was furnished by the French-German TV channel Arte, on July 13, 2000. It broadcast a program called *The Great Fear of Food*, which began by stating that thirty thousand different foods now contain genetically altered soybeans, and fol-lowed with the information that fifty people had died from mad cow disease (BSE). This in turn led to a description of the industrial mass breeding of pigs. Unrestricted con-sumption of meat and its industrial implications were not the subject of the discussion, however. Isolated and unap-petizing aspects of the process were used to attack indus-trial food preparation in general. The scenes from the abattoirs were contrasted with attractive vegetable stands in

Provence. The viewer was made to choose between bloody skulls and handmade cheeses, between protruding guts and ecologically correct vineyards.

What was never mentioned is that there is no parallel between the production of meat and the processing of, say, coffee. Nor can there be any useful comparison between raising pigs on a large scale and making macaroni and cheese in a factory. The latter process is the same as in any private kitchen; only the scale is different. Finally, it is not really helpful to confuse the processes used in the preservation of milk products or in making chocolate with the industrial killing of animals.

Perhaps the most intelligent response to this kind of reporting is to prefer any industrially produced food made of plant materials to meat, that is, pork or chickens, raised by industrial methods. Under an industrial regime, the females are artificially inseminated and reduced to gestation machines. Hogs are artificially fed to reach slaughter weight within a few weeks. Even if they are not actually fed hormones, their food contains additives and flavorings that make them overeat. The fact is, the hogs do not like the animal meal they are fed, which is made of meat scraps and cadavers; chemicals are added to make it more palatable for them.

It is said that you are what you eat. Each of us has to decide how far back in the food chain we want to look before we start eating: to the chop, to the hog, to the animal meal used for fodder, or to the mountains of cadavers that will be made into the meal.

It is a mystery why the vast majority of highly industrial-ized populations do not see the need to have compassion for the animals that are a part of their daily meals. These animals are turned into calories in completely unnatural environ-ments reminiscent of the worst science fiction movies. They are then slaughtered and made into meat and sausages.

As a matter of fact, anyone opposed to industrial animal husbandry should really be in *favor* of industrially prepared foods, which tend to contain little or no meat. Perhaps now is the time to consider more closely the philosophy that is emerging at Nestlé: to stop making processed foods that move through the animal, and to concentrate instead on products that are entirely plant-based.

What we see on television is only part of the battle being waged over industrially prepared food. Its supporters include the food industry, of course, as well as an army of experts in government organizations, technical schools and universities, and trade associations. Their main argument is that food has never been safer or more closely inspected than it is today. This is based on the fact that the incidence of illness arising from industrially prepared foods is extraordinarily low.

Opponents of industrially prepared food include con-sumer and action groups for the protection of nature and the environment, as well as some of the media and other opinion makers. The spectrum of issues they raise is cor-respondingly broad, ranging from food additives and industrial animal breeding to packaging, advertising, and the environment. The latter is at the heart of the current controversy over Nestlé and its use of genetically modified ingredients. Before looking at this subject, however, one must first examine the philosophy of those who object to genetically modified foods.

The critics from the ecological camp generally believe that industrialization was a mistake in our evolution. Its result is that the individual has become alienated from his natural lifestyle and is unable to unfold his true potential. The positive force contrasted with industrialization is always Nature. However, this concept is seldom associated with concrete experiences, such as a walk in the forest or a visit to the zoo. Rather, it is held in almost religious awe, especially by city dwellers.

From this perspective, changing nature is not allowed, and it is always bad. In the over-civilized minds of her advocates, Nature is eternally well-tempered, ever green, a paradisiacal ideal that in fact never existed and never will exist. The reality is that the greatest part of Nature consists of oceans, mountains, deserts, and jungles—environments that are unwelcoming, even life-threatening. This is never mentioned by Nature's urban advocates.

Country dwellers have a very different attitude. For them, the purely useful aspects of Nature are central. In that respect they are no different from Nestlé. "Nestlé is not here to make the world greener," says Nestlé's CEO, Peter Brabeck-Letmathe. "What we are after is creating long-range value. Treating the environment with consideration is simply a part of that plan." The environment is not seen at Nestlé as an abstract ideal, but as a concrete instrument to be used rationally.

The connection between nature and food is demonstrated by the activities of Friends of the Earth (FOE). This organization is the world's largest environmental network, with representation in sixty-one countries. Its sponsors include names like Margaret Atwood, Bruce Cockburn, and Thor Heyerdahl. The foci of its campaigns and programs range from Antarctica to the protection of the oceans, from monitoring international financial institutions to food safety. In England, FOE is one of the leading pressure groups in the environmental arena.

It is in the context of their "Real Food Campaign" that Nestlé becomes a target. "Real food" means nutrients that are free of genetically altered components and so-called poisonous residues. According to FOE, real food has five advantages:

- It is better for your health.
- It frees consumers from the responsibility of spending their money to support businesses that do not care for the planet.
- It is good for animals and the land.
- It creates jobs.
- It creates fair conditions for everyone.

FOE is certain that it is large concerns like Unilever and Nestlé that decide, through their activities on the world market, what is planted or not planted, and where. By not saying where the ingredients in their food products come from, these concerns prevent the consumer from opting for "real food."

According to environmentalists—Friends of the Earth is just one example—industrially produced food is nothing but a substitute for food in its natural state (unground grains, raw milk, live animals), and its quality cannot be compared with "the real thing." To this, Nestlé's answer might be: Our food products are of the highest quality and they are controlled far more rigidly than any food in its natural state ever was. Furthermore, they are made in an environment-friendly way.

It is against this backdrop that the debate over genetically modified ingredients is unfolding. The current state of our knowledge about the effects of adding such components to food is at a level where it is impossible for either opponents or supporters to advance conclusive scientific arguments. For this reason, public discussion of the topic has entered the realm of ethics, addressing such fundamental questions as "Should humankind be allowed to do all the things that we can do?" and "Is it really possible to predict the total, final outcome of our actions?"

This shift in emphasis has involved many groups, including Greenpeace. In its May 2000 issue the magazine *GEO* documented the shift, calling the process a poker game for power, influence, and profit, a masterful maneuver with expert finessing. The *GEO* article details how Greenpeace chose its multinational targets and describes some of its tactics, including mobilizing consumers and even publishing one of the gene technology lobby's strategy papers.

Elenita Dano is a critic who looks at the issue from a different viewpoint. She is an agricultural expert with the Southeast Asian Institute for Community Education (SEARICE) in the Philippines. She considers it extremely unethical for people in rich countries to demand a choice between genetically altered foods and natural foods while recommending that developing countries use gene technology to solve their problems.

Nestlé *is* a supporter of raw materials derived from genetically altered crops, and it employs them in some of its products. This policy has resulted in numerous actions against the Nestlé Group and has assured the corporation a secure place, alongside the makers of genetically altered seeds, among the businesses targeted for boycott.

Despite this pressure, Nestlé refuses to cave in. The company's position remains unchanged: in countries where genetically altered crops are legal and where consumers are willing to accept them, Nestlé will use them. The Netherlands, for example, has a much more relaxed attitude to these things than does Germany. Only 17 percent of the Dutch categorically reject food that contains genetically altered ingredients.

Similarly, in the U.S., two-thirds of Americans support the Food and Drug Administration's position of not requiring labels that identify genetically modified ingredients. Canada also does not require such labeling.

Nestlé's business policy continues to demand that all

products and ingredients be submitted to the strictest internal safety checks. When a Nestlé product contains genetically altered ingredients, it is always clearly marked.

Identifying GM foods can come at a price. In 1998 Nestlé introduced the North American chocolate bar Butterfinger to the German market. It was the first product in Germany to bear the label "Contains genetically modified corn." The product has disappeared from German supermarket shelves because it did not find acceptance among consumers. Whether this was due only to its ingredients or whether Germans did not take to the American-style confection is unclear.

What is clear is that it did not deter Nestlé, although some people inside the company were unsettled. Not so its then CEO Helmut Maucher, who led the charge for GM foods in the 1990s. "I was very provocative on this subject. My own people were shaking whenever I got going...They were worried about their sales. I said something has to be done, someone has to break the ice, and it got broken." Still, Maucher acknowledges the inauspicious start and the reason why. "In a market economy you cannot sell something against the will of the consumer...And when the consumers vote NO, then the product is dead, whether we are Nestlé or anyone else."

Brabeck remains firmly behind GM foods. "We are frequently confronted by the anxiety-producing questions 'What if?' and 'When?' What if genetically altered plants will have been shown to produce higher allergy rates in the population? What if there really are some...that will spread their seeds and cover all the land in a twenty-mile radius?

"The public mind gets overwhelmed by apocalyptic scenarios and succumbs to phrases like 'the dangers of Frankenstein Foods.' Very few voices talk about the risks involved in not using this new technology now, and there is not enough said about the actual and potential advantages of it...What does it mean when a society closes itself off completely from a new form of technology?" Brabeck doubts that this is even feasible, noting that it is an illusion "to believe it is still possible today to build a legal defense wall that will keep genetically modified organisms out."

Maucher is more caustic: "It is much easier to scare people out of their wits with slogans than it is to convince them rationally that this is the only possible way to free 800 million people from chronic hunger. People will not see that gene technology will save water, that it will do exactly the things that the very same sensible ecologists who oppose it want to have done."

Although Nestlé's own research shows that only a small percentage of genetically modified plants are currently being used in human nutrition, Maucher believes that if cloning and genetic alteration can produce a whole range of plants that can be used in preparing food for humans, and if they become cheaper than animal foods, incredible possibilities will open up. "Those who prevent this from happening, who delay this development with their opposition tactics by, say, ten years, will essentially be responsible for the unnecessary deaths of 30 or 40 million people. In this case, good intentions will have produced the opposite of good."

That neatly describes the ethical dilemma that confronts the opponents of gene technology. The number of those who are starving should be being reduced much faster than it is, but today there are no other means to this end than green gene technology. And without some quick and effective alternative, people will continue to starve.

In a conversation, Brabeck again and again seeks to move the topic—and Nestlé's position on it—into a global perspective rather than a merely Western one. "For western Europe, gene technology in agriculture has little or no significance today. We grow so much food that we pay our farmers substantial sums to produce less. We pay vintners to pull up their vines, we pay farmers to destroy their tomatoes, and we pay all around for land to lie fallow. No wonder that in western Europe gene technology, which could increase our harvests or prevent crop damage, is of little interest to anyone.

"For a global enterprise, with global responsibilities, the matter looks entirely different. The picture changes when you look at China or at Africa, where hundreds of millions of people do not have regular, daily nourishment. We have to realize that in those areas, for agriculture to operate in a consistent, long-term framework, it would take more resources than are available.

"With this background knowledge your view changes. And so you will have occasional run-ins. This is explained by the fact of our being a global enterprise, while the activist groups choose their own arenas and targets. But the example of gene technology shows how little power we really have. For power today is mostly power over the public mind. Others have more sway over that than any large firm, such as ours. That is the difference between responsibility and power."

Brabeck believes that the subject of genetically altered food is going to cause bitter debate for many more years. For this debate, however, the general public, as well as its political leadership, tends to be short of knowledge and understanding. Only a realistic technological assessment based on practical experience, Brabeck says, is going to allow us to learn about the risks involved and the best ways to protect ourselves against them.

"As economists, as individuals, and as industrialists," says Brabeck, "we should also ask: What are the risks in blocking this research? What is the risk in handing over a promising line of technological innovation to our competitors? What are the risks in neglecting the technology that could make a substantial contribution in agriculture around the world, and help solve problems that are the responsibility of all of us?"

Norman Borlaug is an agricultural scientist and Nobel Price laureate. The opponents of gene technology love to quote him, and so does Nestlé. This is what he told the General Assembly of the Asian Development Bank: "Extreme environmental elitists seem to be doing all they can to stop scientific progress in its tracks...While affluent nations can afford to pay more for food produced by the so-called 'organic method,' the one billion chronically undernourished people of the low-income, food-deficient nations cannot."

Those who lead global food enterprises also have global responsibilities. In a few years they will be asked not just whether they have maximized shareholder value, they will have to answer more complex questions. Among these will be: What did you do to alleviate hunger in the emerging countries? What was your contribution to research into new and lasting agricultural methods? And what have you done to smooth the way for technologies that can improve crops and yield clearly superior products for your customers?

Brabeck is planning to be ready with the answers. In the meantime, it is corporate policy to enlighten and persuade both governments and the public about the usefulness of gene technology.

The discrepancy between Nestlé's self-image and the claims and challenges of its critics is nowhere more apparent than on the subject of marketing baby food. Here the battle lines are clearly drawn. On the one side stands the International Baby Food Action Network (IBFAN) with its more than 150 member groups in 90 countries. On the other side are Nestlé and numerous governmental institutions, professional organizations, and professional individuals. After twenty years of PR warfare, both sides are having obvious and increasing difficulties in explaining their positions to the public. The enormous body of data and the endless repetition of the same formula-like arguments are in the end less informative than repellent.

The controversy centers on a move by the World Health Organization (WHO) in 1981, when it issued its

International Code for Marketing of Breast-milk Substitutes. IBFAN would later cite UN sources—the WHO and UNICEF are both mentioned—that estimated there were 1.5 million babies dying annually because they were not receiving mother's milk. At the same time these same sources noted that only about half the mothers in the developing countries breast-feed their babies.

While the numbers may be indisputable, the message underwent a subtle change in the statements of IBFAN: "According to UNICEF, 1.5 million babies die annually because they are not breast-fed, but are given bottled baby formula." Only a few words have been added, but they describe a very different situation than the original statement, with respect to both cause and effect. That infants die when they are not breast-fed can have many and varied causes: the death, illness, or undernourishment of the mother, lack of appropriate other foods for the infant, illness, and multiple births. For IBFAN, however, there is only one cause of infant death: bottle-feeding. But bottle-feeding itself does not cause death. Instead, "bottle-feeding" has been substituted for a whole series of causes: poverty, lack of clean water, absence of hygienic measures, and illiteracy.

The original WHO texts describe a reality quite different from that outlined by IBFAN. Witness also the words of the director general of the World Health Organization, Dr. Gro Harlem Brundtland, in a speech she gave on April 19, 1999, in Maputo, Mozambique:

The fate of the newborn is inextricably tied to the health of the mother before and during pregnancy and delivery. Of the more than four million deaths of infants aged less than one month each year, three million occur within one week of delivery, largely as a consequence of poorly managed pregnancies and deliveries. In Africa, each year around two million infants are stillborn or die during the first few days of life. Millions more are crippled by birth trauma and asphyxia during delivery, or suffer lifelong consequences.

The subject of bottle-feeding does not come up in her talk at all, while she does point out all the other circumstances surrounding the baby deaths.

The true causes of infant deaths were also made clear at the Agricultural Summit in Berlin:

Sixteen thousand children die every day as a result of inadequate nourishment. They do not lack calories; they lack protein, vitamins, and minerals. Thirty million babies will be born this year with the symptoms of malnourishment. Hunger met them in the uterus, and they are too small, too thin, too weak to resist disease—they are underdeveloped like the land on which they are born.

Looking at these horrendous numbers—much higher than those reported by IBFAN—one gets the feeling that

IBFAN may have lost touch. It is focusing on a thin slice of the whole spectrum of causes of infant mortality. IBFAN may also have lost sight of the life-saving and health-promoting qualities of mother-milk substitutes, when they are administered in an appropriate way in cases where mother's milk is not available.

Analysis of the positions of the baby-food groups reveals that, from the very beginning, there were several different interests involved. First, there was the basically anti-capitalist stance—a general dislike of large companies. This also includes a tendency to distrust marketing and advertising, which are presumed to be instruments of manipulation. Then there are those who oppose introducing any Western products or lifestyles into the Third World: the enemies of globalization. Then there was the unquestionable fact of children falling ill and dying, and the desire to address this situation.

As we have seen, there are several factors that come together to cause these deaths, but for the sake of simplicity the focus has come to rest solely on the activities of the baby-food industry. The Nestlé boycott is still celebrated as a first, as a high point, as the greatest boycott in the history of NGOs. This was a test of power that is still going on. How far can David force a commercial Goliath to its knees?

The opponents of Nestlé have never been able to prove that the baby-food marketing practices common at the beginning of the 1970s have prevented millions of Third World mothers from breast-feeding their babies. They have never brought forward any concrete evidence that millions

215

of babies died or even fell ill as a consequence of the mothers substituting artificial baby formula for breast milk, or of the wrong or inadequate preparation of these formulas.

There was documentation of individual cases, and this was sufficient to mobilize the public and to pull many well-meaning organizations into the fray, especially those associated with churches. However, neither millions of deaths nor millions of ill children have ever been shown to have resulted from marketing practices. Though critics kept questioning the usefulness of Nestlé baby products, they never sponsored a scientific inquiry into the actual living conditions of Third World babies. The hard-core antagonists were basically interested in the confrontation with Nestlé; the rest was more or less a means to that end.

As this became more evident, many of the other organizations turned away from the cause, which they had taken up only because they had believed they were fighting for children's lives. For these organizations it was enough that various independent institutions had researched the matter and had published their scientific reports, categorically refuting the claims of the action groups. And those organizations that carried out their own monitoring activities in the field were satisfied with their findings as to the true causes of the problem, and were convinced by Nestlé's proofs that they had corrected and improved their marketing practices.

It is undoubtedly true that some mistakes were made in the seventies. To this day the results of these mistakes remain unknown. However, none of this has changed anything in the public presentations of the action groups. Instead of calling it a day, they persist with unproven claims.

The action groups and Nestlé are caught in an impasse from which only mutual agreement could free them. Unfortunately, that is not in the cards at this time. The activists continue to advance their arguments and proofs that Nestlé is bad. In this they have lost sight of the developments that have taken place over the last twenty years. Nestlé believes it is acting in legal ways and continues to document this in statements to the international organizations involved. As its relations with UNICEF show, it is not always successful in these efforts.

On the subject of baby food, Nestlé has not given up, but there is a feeling within the corporation that rational arguments were exhausted a long time ago.

13

The Future of Food
and Nutrition

ESTLÉ'S RESEARCH CENTRE in Vers-chez-les-
Blanc, in the outskirts of Lausanne, Switzerland, is
functional, as are all Nestlé buildings. Various
structures look as if they have been scattered about the
landscape. You could imagine yourself on the campus of a
well-kept but minor university, except that a state-of-the-art
security system reminds you that this is the hub of nutritional research on the planet.

The office of its director (until the spring of 2002),
Andrea Pfeifer, is in the administrative building. Among all
the other nondescript offices, only the sign on her door tells
you she is in charge. Dr. Pfeifer was born in Munich,
worked for a time in the United States, and then moved to
Nestlé. Before she took over as leader of the whole research
complex, she was in charge of the life science sector, where
she and her colleagues developed the foundation of Nestlé's
LCI yogurt product line.

Dr. Pfeifer is familiar with all the arguments that are
advanced against industrially produced foods. She has

dealt with questions about dyes, flavors, and preservatives. "Even my little nephew asks me about flavorings. They learn about things like that in grade school. Of course taste is created by a completely different process, as we are discovering," she explains patiently. Dr. Pfeifer adds that there have been some fundamental transformations in terms of knowledge about food and its components, and how these components function within the human body. Apart from the broadening of scientific knowledge, Dr Pfeifer sees the future of nutrition as being shaped by three other factors:

- changes in consumer behavior in the highly developed countries;
- changes in the nutritional patterns of people in the less developed countries; and
- the fact that food will always remain a fairly conservative product that originates from a limited number of natural sources, and that it is prepared and consumed in a limited number of forms.

Nestlé is in first place within the food industry not just in size, but also with respect to research and development. No other food producer maintains as large a research staff or invests anywhere near the same amount of financial resources. Nestlé now owns a worldwide network of seventeen research stations on four continents. An international workforce of 3,500 people researches and develops innovative products, and works at renewing and improving existing concepts. Year after year Nestlé invests about 1 billion Swiss francs in research and development.

The aim of all this effort is to maintain and strengthen the position Nestlé holds at the cutting edge of the nutrition industry. On the one hand, there are the needs and desires of consumers all around the world, and consumers are becoming more and more knowledgeable and demanding when it comes to the pleasures of food, its convenience, their own well-being, and their health. On the other hand, competition among food producers has grown very intense as a result of globalization. For these reasons, R & D is closely tied to global corporate politics, and is a central part of Nestlé's own activities and corporate culture.

Reliance on research has been characteristic of Nestlé since its founding. Its very first product, was the first formula ever offered for infants, and it was developed through the research of the company's founder. It was the success of this product that led directly to the incorporation of the present business.

When Henri Nestlé retired from the business in 1875, he made sure that the firm would continue his scientific work. At that time the focus was not on developing new products but on making existing products safer. The company hired a scientist whose responsibility it was to develop analytical methods for quality control of milk and grains, the two main raw materials used by Nestlé at that time. As the business spread to other countries, similar laboratories were installed in Nestlé factories around the globe.

The core of today's R & D network was thus established

over a hundred years ago. This network grew over the decades, as Nestlé entered new product areas with its acquisitions. Some of the businesses that joined the Nestlé Group were themselves technological leaders in their respective sectors, such as the Swiss chocolate group Peter, Cailler, and Kohler, as well as the Maggi Group. Both companies were pioneers: Daniel Peter had invented milk chocolate in 1875, and Julius Maggi brought out the first soup cubes in 1908.

Nestlé joined them with the invention of Nescafé, the first powdered coffee, in 1938. This innovation arose from the company's long experience of making dried milk, and it has turned out to be Nestlé's most important discovery ever.

Later acquisitions opened the way to further expansion into canned goods, frozen foods, and pet foods. Most of the new corporations that joined Nestlé brought with them their own R & D components, so that at certain points Nestlé had as many as twenty-five research centers. Such a large and complex collection of activities needed some clear structuring if it was to remain useful, and so the original research facility at Vevey was enlarged in 1950, and later moved to new, central laboratories in neighboring La-Tour-de-Peilz. The latter installation served the company for thirty years, until 1987, when Nestlé inaugurated the new central research center in Vers-chez-les-Blanc.

The current face of R & D at Nestlé emphasizes cooperation and communication between the individual research centers and a keen awareness of the company's business strategies. Liaison with marketing is of course essential, as are contacts with the various Strategic Business Units. The staff at the Vevey head office includes specialists in nutritional law, the environment, intellectual assets, and patents.

R & D at Nestlé rests on four supports: the Nestlé R & D Centres, eight Product Technology Centers, the Adaptation Centers, and Application Groups.

The Nestlé Research Centre (NRC) provides the company with its scientific foundation through basic research into nutrition and the life sciences. It contributes to a better understanding of relevant phenomena in all branches of science related to nutrition, as well as obtaining whatever know-how is required by any of Nestlé's business sectors. The Research Center also supplies scientific knowledge about raw materials, the functioning of the human brain, additives and flavorings, and many other subjects, from botany to molecular biology.

The department of life sciences, for example, is looking for new insights into the process of fermentation caused by yeasts, bacteria, or enzymes, with a view to improving flavor and making them easier to use. On the health front, researchers are looking for new products that will strengthen the immune system or minimize food allergies.

The researchers of the food sciences department also want to understand nature's mechanisms for creating aroma and texture. They seek to develop methods for precise sensory analysis of finished products—simple methods that can be used to define and standardize the sensory experience that a certain food triggers.

Most people, if they stop to think about it at all, assume that the taste they experience is simply a matter of aromatic substances meeting nerve cells inside the mouth and nose. This is not correct, according to the latest scientific findings. Taste is very much a function of tactile sensations within the oral cavity. Whether a food is creamy or slippery, crispy or mushy can cause very different feelings about its quality. To some extent these reactions depend on our expectations of the food in question. Soggy breakfast cereal is as unappetizing as slippery chocolate. Hard pieces of vegetable in soup are experienced as undercooked, not enjoyed as *al dente*. Liquid yogurt does not appeal to those who like it thick.

Finally, in the department of process research, specialists study the technical aspects of the processes used on production lines, such as extraction, extrusion, sterilization, and dehydration. The goal here is to improve them and find better alternatives.

When we speak of industrial food production, it tends to conjure up images of bubbling witches' cauldrons or inhuman, overwhelming machinery reminiscent of Chaplin's *Modern Times*. Neither image is accurate.

Modern food processing means, first of all, creating taste. In a gourmet restaurant, delicious chicken broth does not happen just because a raw chicken is placed in hot water. Food processing also means creating edible food. If you have ever sampled a bad batch of pasta made by hand, you know what that means. A third aim is rendering food germ-free.

Most importantly, perhaps, industrial food production aims at preserving food, whether by drying—the oldest form of food preservation—canning, or freezing. Critics of industrial food often call dried foods "artificial." Yet these foods are particularly kind to the environment, as they need no cooling during storage and thus save energy. Dried foods can also be made when raw ingredients are most plentiful and cheap, and their serving sizes are easier to measure.

Industrial food production involves great quantities, but the processes are essentially no different from those that take place in any kitchen. Industrial cooking resembles more a kitchen of fifty or a hundred years ago, when people still kept stores and cooked things from scratch.

Nestlé's department of nutritional science makes sure, first of all, that all food products meet generally accepted nutritional standards. Its other main purpose is to support the important Strategic Business Unit, Nutrition, in developing new product concepts. New ideas might be for foods that help to maintain bone density, healthy skin, intestinal functions, or cardiovascular health.

The eight Product Technology Centers (PTCs) constitute the second support of Nestlé's R & D work. They deal with the innovation or renovation of the products or processes that lie within the area of activity of each of the Strategic Business Units. The responsibility of the PTCs is to translate scientific ideas into industrial applications.

The Product Technology Centers develop specific technological know-how concerning products, manufacturing processes, and the newest packaging techniques for the part of the Nestlé Group they serve. "A lot of the time we have worldwide technology," says Nestlé USA's Al Steft, and the PTCS translate down to the local market. For example, using a lot of the technology from Skillet Sensations we have introduced a line called Oven Senations because in the U.S. there's a lot of baking that goes on."

At the heart of each PTC is a pilot plant, a sort of miniature factory, where production processes can be tested on a small scale. Reduced-sized models of all the machinery and installations of the product group are there, so that staff can simulate the prototype of any production line, or design new product lines, or make alterations to existing ones. Appropriate workshops support each PTC.

In the test kitchens and tasting rooms of each PTC, experienced professionals sample the sensory qualities of newly developed food products. Each PTC also boasts a "restaurant," where "customers"—either the staff of the Strategic Business Unit or consumers from the area—can be served test meals.

Most Product Technology Centers also include a package development section, since along with each new product, packaging must be created. Consumers want packaging that is attractive and user-friendly. From the technical point of view, however, packaging has a more important task: protecting food from damage that can be caused by light, air, humidity, and bacteria.

Al Stefl cites the example of the repackaging of Coffee-mate, a coffee creamer, as an example of PTC action in this area. "Since its inception, "Stefl observes, "its Been marketed in a brown jar with a screw top. In its liquid form, it was marketed in Gable-top milk cartons. About two years ago we introduced a totally new packaging concept for both of those forms that is so appealing that people want to keep it on their table top."

In addition to all these functions, the Technology Centers also test all aspects of a given product to ensure that they meet Nestlé's own quality standards as well as any regional or local regulations.

The six Research and Development (R & D) Centres constitute the third support of the systems. Like the PTCs, each one of them is dedicated to a specific product area, but they are generally smaller than the PTCs and most often located on the compound or even inside an existing Nestlé factory that manufactures the corresponding products. Three of these six R & D Centres were inaugareted as recently as 2001 and 2002.

The fourth major support of the Nestlé R & D system comprises the two Adaptation Centers, which are located in Singapore and Abidjan (Ivory Coast). The applications developed at these two centers are used far beyond the surrounding regions. Singapore, for example, creates products with a distinctive Asian flavor, which are then manufactured and sold around the world. In Abidjan, the staff works with raw materials available throughout Africa, such as millet, sorghum, cowpeas, and indigenous culinary plants. Both research plants operate on the principle of "do the job where circumstances are most appropriate."

The work of Nestlé's R & D sector is further supported by collaboration with leading, internationally known research institutes and universities. These are chosen for their particular, and highly specialized, knowledge in areas that supplement research done in-house. In the future this co-operative effort will have to be expanded, since modern food products with additional nutritional functions will require clinical testing. These tests will be carried out in both specialized clinics and general hospitals. Research-related collaboration also includes working with the makers of machinery and instruments and the suppliers of raw materials and additives.

R & D creates new products through both innovation and renewal. Nescafé, Maggi cubes, and the range of Nestlé milk products—revolutionary at the time of their introduction—have been and continue to be improved.

Nestlé has over 130 years' experience of making infant food, but the product is still evolving. Consider the company's recently developed hypoallergenic infant formula. By altering one specific protein structure, research has helped substantially to lower the risk of allergic reaction. At the same time, the nutritional content of this product is as close as it can be to that of mother's milk. Worldwide testing of this new hypoallergenic infant formula confirms that it is easier to digest and, thus, better able to meet the nutritional needs of infants.

"Is it true that yogurt is good for you, and if so, why?" That question was the starting point for the research that went into the LC1 product line. The researchers at Nestlé wanted to be sure that the lactic acid bacteria in yogurt effects a positive displacement of harmful intestinal bacteria, and thus supports the immune system. What they found, however, was that 95 percent of the bacteria in yogurt never gets beyond the stomach, but is destroyed there.

Thus began the search for a strain of bacteria that could survive the passage through the human stomach. Researchers looked at all 3,500 bacteria strains cultivated in Nestlé research labs. They based their research on the assumption that the only way milk bacteria can do their job is by getting a good hold on the intestinal walls. Once that happens, their sheer numerical superiority displaces the germs that cause illness.

In 1964 scientists finally identified one strain of yogurt bacteria that meets this criterion: Lactobacillus acidophilus (La1 for short). Tests conducted over the next sixteen years established just how the milk bacteria manage to hang on to the intestinal walls. Researchers also confirmed that La1 multiply well within the digestive tract, are very effective in stimulating the immune system, and can be used in the production of yogurt.

Nestlé did not proceed with the production of LCı until clinical studies in 1991 and 1992 had confirmed earlier findings and certain safety concerns had been satisfied. Nestlé finally marketed LCı yogurt in France. Its label states: "Strengthens the body's natural defenses." Over time, LCı also reached supermarket shelves in many other European countries, as well as in Australia, Brazil, and the Philippines.

LCı is just one result of Nestlé's sustained R & D effort to bring to market food items that promote health and well-being. This aspect of food is becoming ever more important. The company is now doing further research on products that will benefit digestion, the cardiovascular system, skin, bones, and even the health of pets.

Nestlé research also encompasses the creation of new industrial processes. For example, Nestlé pioneered efforts to make low-fat ice cream that boasts the same smooth texture we love in the traditional product. Over the years it has also refined the production of instant coffee with a view to optimizing taste and aroma. Its latest achievement is a special extraction technique that catches the aroma of freshly roasted and ground coffee. This captured scent is then added to Nescafé. Since different blends are marketed in different countries, this enhancement is important in satisfying regional customer expectations.

In the U.S. coffee research takes another form. "What we're focussing on," says Stefl, "are variations of coffee beverages. For example, two years ago, we lauched Nescafé Frothé ... it's highly frothy. It would be more like a cappuccino than a regular coffee."

The R & D technicians at Nestlé have also developed a faster way of making bulk chocolate that does not sacrifice quality. The new method also makes it easier to adapt to regional taste differences.

When Nestlé bought out Rowntree in 1988, the leading product of this company was the candy bar KitKat. Its waffle center was made of a flour so rare that in 1995 it represented only 1 percent of the world's total flour production. This was expensive, but it was impossible to use any ordinary flour because the waffle became too brittle. Nestlé R & D developed a preparation method that permits the use of almost any flour, with no loss of quality. This lowered input costs. More significantly, however, it allowed Nestlé to manufacture KitKat bars in many countries, using locally available flour.

In the United States, Nestlé introduced Skillet Sensations under the Stouffer label, with great success. This easy-to-prepare line of frozen foods only needs to be heated before serving. Again, it was the R & D section of Nestlé that came up with this new way of treating frozen food, which greatly extended the Stouffer product line.

FoodServices is the Nestlé department responsible for large-scale food preparation, and has control of foods and beverages used by restaurants, hotels, airlines, schools, and hospitals. The Product Technology Center that supports FoodServices is located in New Milford, Connecticut. It is staffed by experts in all the appropriate areas, but concentrates especially on nutritional sciences. The products they have developed range from specific ingredients to complete meals. This center also specializes in appropriate packaging and in developing new delivery systems to make products even more convenient and preserve quality.

Nestlé's R & D has also led the way in other areas. Consider the new extraction and dehydration methods developed over the last sixty years for the manufacture of Nescafé. One of the technical innovations that emerged from Nestlé labs was continuous freeze-drying. Indeed, this was one of the twentieth century's most significant innovations in food production, and played a major part in maintaining Nestlé's leading position in several highly competitive market segments.

In the area of powdered milk, Nestlé has been working closely with the makers of the machinery involved, combining its own know-how with the technological and engineering expertise of those companies. This co-operation has led to the development of unique energy-efficient machines. The advantages of these improved production systems devolve to consumers and the environment alike.

The path that Nestlé research follows is determined not only by current product requirements but also by developments in food processing and consumer tastes. The German futurist Gerd Gerken lists ten megatrends for food development in his book *Trends 2015*.

Synthetic Foods. "Food products that are completely synthetic will become widespread because the traditional methods of food preparation will be forgotten." At the present time there are no signs of this happening. There is something called "astronaut food," which is also used by scientific expeditions and the practitioners of extreme sports, but these foods are not appetizing. As well, they are far too expensive at this time to become a trend.

Narcissistic Foods. "Exotic foods will become fashionable and then go out of fashion again, coming and going in waves." This trend has arrived. For the wealthiest population segment, the foods one chooses and the places where they are eaten are a part of one's personal image. Thus, food plays the same role as clothes, cars, watches, and cell phone brands in establishing an individual's personal prestige.

Vegetarianism. This is a classic food trend that never quite goes out of fashion, attracting new converts as external circumstances evolve. The growing reluctance to kill animals for food may be more significant in the current growth of this trend than arguments based on ethical considerations and health concerns. Any vegetarian who does not know how to cook and does not wish to live on raw foods will, however, reach for the appropriate industrially prepared foods.

Grazing. "Not eating clearly defined major meals, and instead, consuming a series of between-meals small snacks." This trend has become a fast-growing business under the name food-on-the-move. People no longer set aside special times for eating their three meals a day; they eat when it is possible, fitting it in alongside their other activities. Breakfast is eaten on the way to work, lunch is combined with jogging, dinner with a break before the movie. The food industry is ready for this trend with packaged snacks and automatic dispensers.

Consumer Power. "With all their many ambitions and faddy attitudes, consumers will increasingly be the *creators* of foods." This trend has become part of the language of all those sectors of the economy where the "prosumer" is recognized. What prosumers want dictates what certain producers make in the short run. Product adaptations range from ice cream flavors to the colors of car enamel.

The New Honesty. "We will realize the collective daydream of honest, unadulterated, clean food." This trend is encountered most clearly in the products of and promotions for so-called "slow-food," and by the practitioners of biodynamic farming. These farmers market their produce themselves. The food industry is not worried about this trend since it only a small part of the total market.

Brain Food. "Foods that stimulate inner visions and fantasies." Today the term "brain food" is understood to mean foods and substances that enhance intellectual performance. In my own opinion, computers, television, and discotheques can supply better visions and more fully realized fantasies.

Neo-Raw Food. "Transfiguring of raw, untreated foods ... a sort of high-tech anti-processing, an artificially created naturalness." This trend is only a variant of the New Honesty. In Japan, where fish is often eaten raw, freshness is of course a necessity. There is also a Japanese fashion for growing vegetables in a completely aseptic environment; you don't wash them unless you are trying to add germs to your food.

High-tech Nature. "Synthetically made aromas and preservatives will become more and more important in human nutrition." This is true because people want to enjoy every conceivable taste sensation, irrespective of time and place. All imaginable aromas are, therefore, being made today: broiled chicken, crab, even rat bouillon!

Pop Food. "Food as a part of an evening's entertainment." When eating becomes an event, when what matters is an interesting venue within the framework of "entertainment," catering is quickly at hand to offer various convenience foods. Just like in the home, convenience foods are handy in the hospitality industry, and especially in the growing Experience Hospitality industry, that is, restaurants where eating is marketed as an event.

As we can see, many of these "future trends" are already a part of everyday life. Yet despite these futuristic concepts and the changes in consumer behavior, the fundamentals of nutrition do not change.

Each Nestlé product starts with raw materials made by nature, including coffee, cocoa, milk, soybeans, and grain.

During the 130 years of its existence Nestlé has accumulated an extensive body of knowledge about the treatment and uses of each raw material. This enables Nestlé to transform these materials into more attractive and healthful products, corresponding to consumer tastes and desires.

In the future, consumers can expect more products that make positive contributions to their health. This does not mean, however, that food is going to be turned into medicine. Nestlé's first probiotic products have already shown that good health and good taste can go hand in hand. Future products—the fruits of R & D—are expected to help with diabetes, osteoporosis, obesity, cardiovascular disease, and flabby skin. Even brain function will in future be supported by foods, as our knowledge of the connection between diet and mental activity becomes clearer.

While examining trends is informative, food must be judged by the present reality, not future prospects. Of course, food quality is subject to legal regulations, trade agreements, and hygienic or public health standards. But the features of food that contribute to the satisfaction of consumers create many other criteria from the food producer's viewpoint:

- physiological aspects of foods, such as their nutritional value and other health-promoting qualities
- convenience, enjoyment, sociability potential
- sensory qualities, including taste, consistency, aroma, composition, color, and appearance

- price and affordability, as well as the relation between price and quality

The most difficult thing about developing a new food product is that it is not enough to concentrate on one or even a few of the above features. Even the safest, most wholesome, and most affordable of foods is rejected by consumers if it is not attractive. Foods that people are not used to eating will also have a hard time gaining acceptance.

Understanding the five senses, as well as an accurate knowledge of regional or national cuisines, is a must when it comes to satisfying customers worldwide and gaining or maintaining a lead over the competition. For this reason Nestlé has adjusted its basic research and its technology in order to optimize the sensory qualities of its entire range of products.

Originally, Nestlé's laboratories were set up primarily to maintain strict quality control over the entire manufacturing process, from raw material to end product. Today such controls are standard not just at Nestlé but everywhere. Nevertheless, consumers have not given up their suspicious stance towards industrially made foods, and unfortunate occurrences can always take place. Among these we have seen contamination of beverages in returnable bottles, maggots in fresh fish, and BSE-infected beef. But these events are completely unrelated or only marginally connected to the large-scale industrial production and distribution of food products. Over the last thirty years, methods of food analysis have improved dramatically.

Together with governments and trade associations, Nestlé makes every effort to provide the public with scientifically correct facts.

Although Nestlé does not grow any of its own raw materials, it does take responsibility for their production, from the seeds through fertilization to harvest, and beyond that, to transport and storage. This applies also to all animal products used by the corporation. A global network of regional and international control labs ensures that any potential risks are immediately eliminated. In the Nestlé Research Centre, about one-quarter of the staff of six hundred work in the Department of Quality and Safety Control, which is in constant contact with all Nestlé branches.

The state-of-the-art laboratories conduct their research according to the latest internationally accepted methods and standards. Globally respected agencies for food safety legislation, such as the Food and Drug Administration in the United States, acknowledge the high standards Nestlé maintains in the area of microbial and toxicological food safety.

This long-standing credibility is reflected in the Nestlé seal of quality. Since most of the corporation's products bear this seal, a problem with any one of them—even the smallest flaw—would have immediate deleterious effects on the credibility and acceptance of all Nestlé products. This seal of quality is no mere promise to consumers; it binds the *corporation* as well. As a multinational, Nestlé is much more widely affected by negative publicity than it would be if the corporation's products were merely local brands, acting independently in different, widely separated markets. Consumer concerns therefore take on a global nature in terms of both quality and comfort/convenience.

In terms of quality, the most important aspect now and looking forward is healthfulness. Foods can help prevent illness; people who eat well are better equipped to battle illness. This sounds simple in theory, but in practice it is not. Each health-promoting additive must have a food item to deliver it. Finding the appropriate food is a challenge in itself, as is finding the right substances to add, quantifying them, and predicting how long each will remain effective.

There is a big difference between the way people take medicine and the way they take nutrients. We take drugs because we are aware that we are ill. Medicine is given in the form of pills, tablets, capsules, or drops, and exact directions accompany them: "Half a tablet with water, three times daily, before meals."

Food is not taken like that. Nestlé likes to show this by the use of a real-life example. It was suggested to the corporation that, in the Third World, Maggi soup cubes should be enriched with minerals and vitamins. The idea was that since soup cubes are a basic food, if enriched, they could help reduce certain nutritional deficiencies in the population. In principle this idea seemed promising, but after testing was carried out by Nestlé, it turned out to be impracticable.

Maggi soup cubes are very widely used in Africa, but they are employed as a seasoning, and so are consumed in minute quantities. Their consumption would have had to increase considerably in order to relieve any vitamin deficiencies. However, if people started to consume more for that purpose, they would end up ingesting unhealthy amounts of salt and spices. It was concluded that changing general eating patterns would be more effective and safer than altering Maggi soup cubes, no matter how convenient a vehicle their popularity makes them appear.

Chocolate too would seem an ideal carrier for healthful additives, but it is psychologically unsuitable, especially in the highly developed countries, where it is considered a "sweet" and "fattening." Few people would follow directions that read: *Eat two chocolate bars every day.*

So the food that serves as carrier for the active substance is in some ways more important than the substance itself. Nestlé is in the enviable position of having many convenient carriers to choose from: milk products, yogurt, cereals. These foods are eaten on a daily basis. In the future it will matter less who invents the active ingredients, the pharmaceutical or the food industry; what will matter is what carrier consumers prefer.

Today, the range of so-called functional foods is already quite substantial. From isolated nutritive substances through dietary additives all the way to specially designed foods, such as probiotic milk products, this range offers something for every purse and many needs. The rising cost of health care and the aging of the population support the trend towards functional food.

Fortunately, the relationship between a natural biochemical structure in food and its effect on health is something that is easier and easier to explore. Consumer interest in health-promoting foods is becoming intense, and so is the general confusion they are causing. The new concepts alone are enough to baffle the uninitiated: designer foods, pharma-foods, functional foods, nutraceuticals. The first two were developed primarily for bodybuilders and athletes; the others are of interest to the general public.

Functional foods are generally understood to be food products that "have been modified by the addition of nutrients or additives so as to deliver certain specific healthful benefits or advantages." In Japan, where functional foods originated, an even more precise definition is used: functional foods are nutrients (not capsules, tablets, or powders) that are based on natural ingredients. They are and should be eaten as part of the daily diet. They have defined functions, which may include the following:

- improving immune-system functioning
- prevention of specific diseases
- support in recovering from specific illnesses
- control of physical and psychological ailments
- slowing of the aging process

A conference of experts, convened by the Japanese department of health as far back as 1988, recommended the legalization of functional foods. Since then, about 350 firms have become active in the field; total business volume is more than $3 billion. As yet, Western food producers can only dream of this level of consumer appeal, but the growing number of functional food products points in this direction.

According to the Japanese ministry of health, nutraceuticals are foods with medicinal or healthful additives. These can be isolated nutrients, dietetic additives, or genetically developed "designer nutrients." The range of additives includes fiber, oligosaccharides, sugar alcohols, amino acids, peptides and proteins, glycoside, alcohols, isoprenoides and vitamins, choline, milk acid bacteria, minerals, unsaturated fatty acids, phytochemicals, and antioxidants.

There is no doubt that some of these substances have beneficial effects on the physiology of the body. Polyunsaturated fatty acids can be added to the list as well. Fish oils are also under study at this time, as some of them seem to have therapeutic effects on arteriosclerosis and chronic inflammatory diseases. The health-promoting effects of fiber have been well known for a long time.

The group of phytochemicals includes all substances that occur naturally in plants; they are also known as secondary plant substances. Usually the term refers only to those elements that are biologically active in the plants themselves, such as dyes, chemicals that fight intruders or illnesses, and those that regulate plant growth. Unlike carbohydrates, fiber, proteins, and fats, the phytochemicals play no part in primary human digestion; they have no nutritional value for humans. They occur in tiny quantities, they differ widely from each other, and their effects are pharmacological. A mixed diet delivers about 1.5 grams of phytochemicals daily, and this small amount may comprise five to ten thousand different substances. They influence our food preferences as carriers of specific tastes and odors.

The health benefits of phytochemicals are extremely varied. They can be anti-cancerous or antioxidant, modulate the immune system, regulate blood pressure and blood sugar levels, be anti-microbial, anti-thrombotic, and anti-inflammatory, lower cholesterol, and promote digestion.

The benefits of probiotica and prebiotica foods are also worth noting. Fermented milk products were sold in European pharmacies as far back as the turn of the last century, to combat intestinal infections that frequently resulted from badly stored foods. Today you can buy yogurts that are labeled "probiotica," and some contain additional "prebiotica." The difference between these products and ordinary yogurt is that, whereas milk bacteria are responsible for fermentation in all yogurt, in the probiotic products they play an additional role: the number of living bacteria grows after the yogurt is eaten, so that there is a good chance some will survive and settle in the intestines.

Probiotica, then, can be defined as substances, containing living micro-organisms, that can be taken orally and are meant to change the balance of the intestinal flora so as to make it beneficial to overall health. Prebiotica are ingestible parts of food products that are there to enhance the growth or activity of one or more strains of micro-organisms in the intestines, in order to produce a positive effect on the body.

The most commonly used yogurt bacteria are Lactobacillus bulgaricus and Streptococcus thermophilus. Many probiotic products also contain Lactobacillus acidophilus or L. casei. The significant difference between the bacteria is that some perish in the same lactic acid that they themselves produce; they cannot live in the low pH environment they create. Other bacteria strains are acid-resistant. The latter can reach the large intestine despite the extremely acidic environment of the stomach and small intestine, where salts from the gall bladder and proteolytic enzymes create acidity. Only bacteria that have made the passage through the stomach and small intestine can have any probiotic effects on the body.

Critics of the food industry have said that though the tag line "A daily addition to your health" sounds promising, there is no unbroken chain of proof that it is true. It has also been suggested that probiotic yogurts are not really new nutritional items. The critics also claim that of the common bifida bacteria, 30 percent tend to reach the small intestine alive, while of the new strains it is still only 40 percent that succeed. Nonetheless, food producers have invested in the marketing of these products. Nestlé alone put $16 million into advertising LC1.

In many Western countries the laws distinguish sharply between foods and medical products. For this reason no food producer may make any claims concerning the health benefits of its products, no matter how well these may be documented by science. Nestlé could respond to its critics with some persuasive arguments in favor of its products, but if successful, the result of its efforts would be that Nestlé yogurt could only be sold by prescription. Clearly, those who drew up the existing laws simply never imagined the day when food would be seen to make you healthy as well as satisfy your hunger.

14

A Question of Taste

NUTRITION RUNS IN TANDEM with taste. And in the final analysis, taste is what matters most to consumers. Nestlé and its rivals are in the business of satisfying this basic need. Many people insist that the foods of their own culture are the *right* foods. They opine that people in other parts of the world only eat differently prepared foods because they are too poor to get the real stuff. But people all over the world believe this, so clearly it cannot be correct.

In West Africa, for example, rat bullion is a very popular Maggi product. Naturally, for many good reasons, the cubes do not contain any rat meat at all, but they do have the desired rat taste. Rats are a delicacy that is not served every day. Since rats cannot be bred, they have to be hunted. They are not always available, and this fact alone would make their industrial processing very difficult. There are also hygienic and health reasons for not eating rats. But since rats have an intense, gamy aroma, which is appreciated by Europeans as well, it was no big thing for

Nestlé to lend some of its African bouillon cubes that special flavor.

Africans traditionally use bouillon cubes with an onion flavor when they cook monkey or bat. Maggi offers products appropriate to these dishes as well, and they are very successful.

The bouillon markets of Africa function very much like the markets of Europe did after World War II; the only difference is the taste dimension. In postwar Germany, chicken did not constitute everyday fare because it was so expensive; it would appear on the table only on Sundays, if at all. The demand for chicken stock was commensurately high, as it offered an affordable variant of the unavailable delicacy. When chickens started to be bred on a massive scale, they became cheaper and were therefore valued less highly. Today, beef bouillon has replaced chicken stock as the favorite Maggi product in both Germany and Switzerland. The markets of eastern Europe and Russia, by contrast, are chicken-bouillon markets. In the Ukraine, for example, chicken is still relatively expensive because professional chicken breeding does not exist there.

Of course, not all bouillons are the same, nor is bouillon used the same way everywhere. In South America, it is used in cooking rice. In order to keep the rice light in color, the bouillon has to be very clear. And while in European bouillons little pieces of parsley are absolutely essential, they would be completely out of place in South America, because they would make the rice look contaminated.

If one of Nestlé's branches were unable to satisfy the expectations and tastes of local consumers, its products would soon pile up in the warehouse. And this is not purely a matter of flavor. The way foods are prepared and the raw materials used also differ from place to place, often quite substantially. In Asia, for example, there is no common standard for food preparation, and the Adaptation Center in Singapore must therefore meet a very wide range of customer expectations.

All the different markets are watched over by so-called Application Centers, which are responsible for the quick adaptation of products to changing circumstances, such as shifts in the supply of raw materials. They also react to evolving market conditions, such as the successful introduction of a new flavor by the competition or the sudden availability of previously scarce packaging materials.

Sometimes there are tiny details that need to be corrected. One example might be tomato flakes, which cause problems when the tomatoes are obtained from a new grower who planted a different strain. As a result, small adjustments have to be made in the process of preparing the flakes. Another task of the application group is line extension, that is, the widening and adaptation of the range of products in response to local conditions.

What is changed is not the fundamental process of preparing the products, but their general presentation. Thus a pancake has to be different in Austria than in Germany. There are about ten thousand ingredients that can be combined to create something like twenty thousand different food products.

The habits of consumers do meet in certain food categories, but on closer inspection even these tastes are much less universal than they appear to be. It is specifically the products that do not stem from any particular cuisine that have found general acceptance: McDonald's is enjoyed everywhere, as is Coca-Cola.

Coffee is a different matter entirely. There is no such thing as a European coffee. In the Mediterranean countries, people like coffee with a dark roast and a strong body. Consumers in Germany prefer a lighter roast and a milder, slightly tart taste.

The differences outweigh the similarities. Thus, there is no standard recipe for European tomato soup. In France they like a thick, creamy concoction, while in Germany they prefer a thin broth with tomato pieces in it.

Nestlé sells about four thousand individual products in Europe, and of these, fewer than one hundred are identical throughout the continent. In western Europe not even the preferred taste of chocolate is uniform, even though most everybody likes After Eight, Smarties, and Lion chocolates. Only pets have no regional preferences.

There are even regional tastes for cereals. Certain kinds of cornflakes are preferred over others in particular places. And if you think that baby foods and pabulum cater to a completely untrained palate, think again. After all, it is not the babies that do the shopping. And when they sample their baby's food, mothers want to meet with a taste they themselves are familiar with. For this reason, puréed carrots are prepared according to different recipes; in France, for example, they like a more salty taste than elsewhere.

Food, then, is not expected to be just wholesome. It must also taste "right," or as people say everywhere, "like my mother would make."

Regional differences are especially marked with culinary products, of which Maggi flavoring is a typical example. In France there actually exists a Maggi flavoring border, which runs through the Lorraine. Maggi flavoring is used in Germany, Austria, and Switzerland, and also in Poland, the Czech Republic, and Slovakia. Thus in all the formerly German areas, Maggi is still used, but sometimes only a few kilometers west, in a French-speaking town, Maggi flavoring would under no circumstances be considered an acceptable condiment.

Bouillon cubes, which might seem to be a fairly straightforward product, have to be adapted to national expectations everywhere. In eastern Europe, chicken broth is supposed to be dark; in western Europe it is light and golden. The eye participates in the enjoyment. Even things like mayonnaise involve many regional changes. In Germany, Thomy mayonnaise is slightly sweet, in Switzerland, slightly tart.

LC1 Go drink is one of those new products that are able to cross the borders of regional taste, but regular yogurt is not free to move about. In some places consumers like it best when it is easy to stir, like French yogurt; in other places they prefer the more solid German kind that makes the spoon stand up.

Russian chocolate is a whole subject unto itself. It has to

be dark and slightly bitter. In Russia, milk chocolate with a delicate melt is not considered a quality product. It is also not a widely known fact that the Russians are among the most avid consumers of ice cream in the whole world. Nestlé is the leading ice cream maker in the Russian market.

Taste is an extremely complex phenomenon. Our tastes are formed by the foods we are exposed to. Other important factors are tradition, cultural heritage, and religion. Idiosyncratic features come into it as well, including allergies. And psychological factors may play a role. For example, you may lose your appetite for eel if you happen to observe the way they are caught with the head of a bullock (as is described in great detail in Günter Grass's *The Tin Drum*). Our tastes change over the course of our lifetime, and men and women taste things differently. Our taste preferences are partly a product of our body's wisdom, as it tries to guide us towards foods that provide for current physical needs.

What is consumed, where, and how are not under the control of any industry, and even less under that of a single corporation. It is true that supply and demand influence one another. The supply of food items is getting steadily broader because people love change, and because cooking trends are adapting to an international lifestyle. Regional preferences, however, remain. Pizza tastes different in Germany than in Italy, and on German dinner tables, Chinese food loses most of its traditional variety.

Worldwide, the many different variations and orientations of taste remain intact. American children would not enjoy a traditional Japanese breakfast of cold rice, pickled vegetables, and raw fish, even though it might give their taste buds good training. It is not the local Nestlé branch that decides what will be eaten but the consumers. Nestlé maintains an extensive network of branches so as to be able to win over consumers with the largest possible array of offerings.

If consumers' diets are less balanced and duller than some food gurus think they should be, we ought not to look at the food industry for the source of the problem. Food mirrors social conditions and developments. Of course, it is possible that changing foods might alter social patterns. We will have to wait and see what the future brings.

Index

Index

Index

Index